Open your eyes . . .
Face the truth!

Open your eyes . . .
Face the truth!

I. L. Jackson

Copyright © 2003, 2004, 2008, 2013, and 2016 by: Iran L. Jackson

ISBN # 978-0-6152-3798-5

This book was printed in the United States of America.

Fifth Edition, 2016

To order additional copies of this book, go to;

Lulu.com, book listing 2307374

Or send an email to **andastheywent@gmail.com**

This book is dedicated to my wife Charlita, my daughter LaShara and son Iyran.

I love you!

Contents

Introduction

August 1998, I was on the southbound New Jersey Transit train, heading home to Philadelphia. I had just been fired from MTV (in New York) where I worked as a Production Artist doing layouts and backgrounds in their animation department. I was reading the Bible, trying to figure out how I was going to tell my wife the bad news. I was reading the book of Ezekiel and came to these words in the third chapter, seventeenth verse, *"Son of man, I have made you a watchman . . . and therefore hear the word at my mouth, and give them warning from me."* The words seemed to leap off the page! I read the words over and over again. But *what* is a *"watchman"* and *who* was I to warn; and *what* was I warning people about? I did some poking around and found out that a *'watchman'* is a guardian, one who warns and protects others against impending danger.

Within a week's time I had found employment at the local CVS Pharmacy as a *'watchman'*—whose job was to patrol the store and discourage shoplifters. This could not be what God meant when he told me that He has made me a *"watchman"*.

Two months later, while visiting a friend at his place of employment, I was asked, *"Are you looking for a job?"* by one of his coworkers. I applied and was hired at the Philadelphia Anti-Drug/Anti-Violence Network (PAAN) and began working as a Prevention Specialist soon after. As a Prevention Specialist I was *sent* to dozens of schools and recreation centers around the city, warning youth (K-12th grades) against drug abuse, violence, (negative) peer pressure and various other topics. **God *had* made me a watchman!**

I didn't realize I was writing a book! I was merely typing out presentations to put into a folder so that I would not have to rewrite them over and over again. (I learned from a good friend and coworker to jot down any important points I desired to make on the back of a business card before each presentation). Before I knew it I had nearly 100 pages (typed)!

What I have written is the result of the insights, observations and experiences derived from my interactions with countless youth (as well as my own life). I pray that this book will be a blessing to you!

Open your eyes!

(Hey yo…!) I don't do drugs; don't claim to be a thug!
Don't get high—don't "puff lah"
My only limit is the sky! That's no lie…
I'm still *"fly"!*
I'm cool—like a winter storm…
But play it safe like I'm in a parked car—with my seatbelt still on!
Me fight, it's not likely…
I'm with the "Peace Posse"!
We "Do the Right Thing"—like Spike Lee!
That means—we carry no guns and knives.
We bring the 411, plus we're saving lives!
Giving you the straight truth—and exposing lies…
…we're being programmed to fail—but y'all don't realize!
So what has TV and radio been teaching you?
Do drugs, curse and shoot—or maybe be a prostitute?
Yo! Sex, drugs and violence corrupt…
…enters us and builds up, causing us to self-destruct!
Wonder why so many brothers carry Glocks and "9's"?
It's because they've seen "Scar Face" too many times!
It's because they've heard guns "praised" in too many rhymes!
It's 'cause those who live in darkness—don't know that they're blind!
They desire to be like criminals they admire…
…solve problems with gunfire, death or prison's how they retire!
Are you a thug selling "weed" and "dust"?
Guess what? Guess who you're worshipping?
"Greed" and "Lust"! Oh! You're mad?
You're thinking, *"I'm gonna beat him up!"*
Well, it's the "truth!" Do you want to get 'free' or what?
Young eyes have seen too many violent scenes…
…broadcast not just on TV—but smart phone screens.
Causing violent minds that write violent 'rhymes'…
…and do "violent acts", creating "violent times"!
Yo! A man kills when evil thoughts build…
And a mother cries as her young son dies…
Open your eyes!

Written by: I. L. Jackson

Fear

We live in the era of reality TV. Most of us have seen or heard of the show Fear Factor, and many may even be loyal fans. Each week (daily if you have cable or satellite TV or access to social media), many of us witness both men and women subjecting themselves to various (often humiliating and disgusting) stunts: being buried in a tub of worms, snakes, or scorpions; being made to jump off of moving helicopters or planes into huge stacks of cardboard boxes; and being challenged to collect small flags from moving vehicles or scaffolding and to be dropped bungee-jump style off of buildings in cars. We've even witnessed contestants bobbing for plastic rings in tanks of cows' blood, chucking frozen rats across the room into buckets, and even to the passing of ground up animals and insects from the mouth of one partner to another in order to fill a large container. Jerry Seinfeld said it best, "That's not reality TV." At least none of the things mentioned above happens in my reality, and I am willing to wager that they are not a part of your everyday reality either!

However, we all have fears; and while the show mentioned above may be short on reality, it does force us to face those things that we are most afraid of (or those things that are most disgusting to us).

As a society, we seem to have a love affair with the things that scare us. Many of us get a thrill from things that cause fear, not realizing how much these things tend to affect us! Adrenaline junkies "face their fears" by plunging off buildings with parachutes, diving off high cliffs and such. Others like to take in all of the latest horror and "slasher" flicks (which desensitize them to the increasing violence and grisly deaths that happen around them daily). Many laugh at deaths, accidents and calamities (things that should make us respond with grief and compassion)

This author was watching Star Wars Clone Wars cartoon one day — (er… what can I say, this author is a big kid at heart) and heard Lord Duku (Jedi Knight, who became a traitor to the Dark Side), state to his apprentice; *"You must have fear, surprise, and intimidation on your side. If any of one these elements is lacking…retreat… You must break them before you engage them. Only then will you have victory…"* This is how the enemies of our destinies—whoever those enemies happen to be—keep us bound to their way of thinking, trapped in circumstances, paralyzed (with fear) from moving out or leaving unhealthy environments and people, and neutralized, never achieving our dreams and goals.

What is fear?

Fear- an unpleasant feeling of anxiety or apprehension caused by the presence or anticipation of danger - Encarta Dictionary: English (North America)

Fear is <u>not</u> (always) bad or wrong! In fact, *fear* can be a safety mechanism:

- To prevent one from touching fire or getting too close to it
- To prevent one from running into a busy street or highway
- To cause one to be alert around certain animals and people
- To prevent one from wandering into dangerous places and situations (like certain neighborhoods known to be violent or—even into a shoot-out)

Fear can be explained as an anxious concern:

- As a mother fears for her child's safety crossing the street or walking to school for the first time
- As a father fears for his son's well-being during a little league game
- As one who does a job or performs a task and must present it to a teacher or supervisor for a grade or approval

There are three reactions to fear:

*(The following information is provided by Christian Education Ministries and Training, Dr. Walter Swinson, president)

- Foolishness (the daredevil or like the videos "Jack-Ass")

  o Having no respect for dangerous situations—Small children do not know any better; they have yet to learn. However, there are some who walk or leap headlong into trouble, not having an

understanding of consequences (trying stunts without planning or protection; being fired for jumping in the boss's face; suspended or expelled for threatening the teacher and or principal; trespassing and falling; or having something fall on them, being burned, crushed, or shot)
- o Having no fear of injury to self or others—willing to put self and others in danger (like one who is high on drugs/alcohol and is allowed to drive or operate machinery)

- Cowardice (the victim)

  - o Running from or avoidance of conflicts or stressful situations
  - o Won't stand up for self
  - o Runs or retreats when picked on or challenged in some way

- Courageous (the brave)

  - o Having and acknowledging fear yet continuing to move forward despite one's feelings, willing to face and confront fear

Fear is the *root* cause and the beginning of a great many of our issues! Because fear is spread in so many ways and has so saturated our lives, we (all) have been hindered, even blinded, unable to see who we really are. Therefore, we are unable to reach our full potential. A child is born without an awareness of fear, but he/she learns through what is seen, heard, taught and experienced.

If a person is never told of his/her potential, who he/she is or what that person can achieve, that person's peers, circumstances, and surroundings may introduce fears that may keep him/her from striving toward success. That person learns to live or exist in fear.

Fear is a root of the following:

- Stress/ anxiety/worry—fear that something will go wrong, will not be good enough, will fail or be rejected
- Depression—caused by worry or anxiety
- Low self-esteem—worry, anxiety, and depression about one's appearance, intelligence and about not having clothing or material things (that others

have) that have taken root, causing one to think of one's self as a failure or having less worth than one's peers

- Unforgiving—fear of being hurt, dissatisfied, disappointed, or used (again) develops into resentment or bitterness
- Anger/rage—resentment or bitterness that is acted out (verbally or physically)
- Distress—fear that one's situation will never change or get better (hopelessness)
- Paralysis—intense fear which causes the body to freeze in place, becoming immobile:
    o Fear of failing—You are worried that you will not be good enough (true success is rarely achieved on the first try and nobody is perfect)
    o Fear of embarrassment or of being laughed at—it's inescapable! We all do embarrassing things from time to time. That's why "America's Favorite Home Videos" is such a popular show! We must learn not to take ourselves so seriously.
    o Fear of being seen as stupid or incompetent—No one is good at everything, and no one is bad at everything. Fear of rejection— We all desire to be accepted to be liked and to have friends
    o Fear of being hurt—As long as we are on the planet Earth, someone, somewhere, and somehow is going to hurt our feelings, and we will from time to time (whether we intend to or not) hurt others. However, whatever doesn't kill us makes us stronger (and we should not blame everyone for the insensitivity of a few!)

Because of the fears listed above, many of us are hindered from doing the following:

- Getting better grades
- Building or maintaining strong friendships or relationships
- Realizing our own self-worth, uniqueness and style
- Setting and achieving higher goals and working toward them
- Getting to know people of other races and cultures . . . the list goes on

Fear can be rational or irrational!

- Rational fear—concern over something that can really cause harm (fear of fire for instance)
- Irrational fear—anxiety that stems from one's imagination or fear without cause (fear of people, of going out into public places, or of objects that do not provoke fearful reactions in others)

Persistent irrational fear is called a phobia!

One who has a phobia disorder has become so gripped with fear that one is unable to function normally. Once again, one may have a fear of certain objects or situations (like statues, heights, or being in small or enclosed spaces). One might be intensely fearful of germs or afraid to go outside or into public places, and so on.

Fear has been described in several ways:

*F*alse *E*vidence *A*ppearing *R*eal!

(Or we can . . .)

*F*orget *E*verything *A*nd *R*un!
(I have heard of other variations; however, these are enough.)

We all have fears!

We all experience anxiety or panic attacks, which come upon us suddenly, overwhelming us with feelings of loneliness, depression, and isolation. But we do not have to dwell there. We can fight that feeling! We can choose to respond to our fear rather than to react out of fear.

The difference between responding and reacting is this: responding is acknowledging that we are fearful, yet we do not allow fear dictate our actions; reacting out of fear is letting what we are afraid of have control over us and how we act.

Fear seems to be the one demon (if you will) that keeps us from discovering who we really are, our true worth, and what we can accomplish!

What causes fear?

(The following information is provided by Christian Education Ministries, Dr. Walter Swinson)

- Traumatic experiences
    - Being hurt or injured (breaking a bone, getting stitches)
    - Experiencing abuse or neglect (being tortured, starved, etc.)
    - Seeing violence, abuse, and or death (also from watching these things on TV, movies, reading books, etc.)

I remember seeing Jaws as a small child; I'm still afraid of (deep) water to this day!

- Parents who display excessive fear
    - Excessive concern of others' opinions (appearance, dress, tidiness—how things look is extremely important to them)
    - Being overly protective—the parents attempt to shield their child or children from life's hurts and disappointments; however, this only makes their children handicapped when the parent is no longer able to be their children's "crutches."

- The use of scare tactics (various threats, imaginary creatures, and circumstances as a method of warning, teaching, or controlling)
    - "If you do that, then the Boogeyman will get you!"
    - "Don't go there, or the people there will do something bad to you!" (Have you seen the movie The Village?)
    - "If you tell, I will hurt you or your family!" (What images come to your mind at the hearing of these words?)

- An undeveloped or underdeveloped sense of self-worth

    Like in the story "The Ugly Duckling," many of us walk about fearful and feel rejected because we are not like our peers. We are constantly teased and picked on, bullied and belittled. Perhaps it is because we truly are different! Perhaps we are of a whole other breed, a higher and more beautiful type of person, whose purpose in life is not to be that of our current (average) peer group. We must recognize that we are different, that we are special, and that our worth is great! Then we must seek out those who have been where we are and are going in the direction we desire to go. Like the Ugly Duckling, once he saw others, who looked like him and realized how beautiful he was, he immediately left those average ducks and joined the swans! We too must do this!

- Emotional overload
  o Denying one's own feelings
  o "I can't. I shouldn't or I have no right to feel like this."
  o "I must not look soft; these feelings are for the weak."
  o "I can't let people see me like this, they might laugh."

- Holding on to stress
  o Holding on to anger or hurt
  o Unforgiving (fear of being hurt or offended again)
  o Never expressing or releasing feelings of anxiety or pressure

(Sickness and disease such as high blood pressure, ulcers, heart attacks and more can be linked to stress/fear that has been internalized.)

- Being raised in a household where strictness or perfection is strongly enforced
  o All things must be just so
  o There is no room for error

- People pleasing
  o In order to be accepted
  o To fit in with a group
  o To be seen as cool

(This is a major reason for young people joining gangs and engaging in other negative behaviors.)

Avoiding conflicts, the unfamiliar, or stressful situations involves one's ability to grow, how one interacts socially, and how one helps to build up one's confidence and self-esteem. A person who is unwilling to face this fear will continue to be imprisoned by it. One's thought patterns will become increasingly negative, even suspicious, fearing that everyone is out to get him or her. This is called paranoia. This thinking is linked to the following:

- Runaway imagination
  - o Always assuming the worst about everything
  - o Believes that there will never be a change in one's self, one's circumstances, or in other people

This is called hopelessness, and it is truly a sad and dangerous state. Proverbs 29:18 of the Bible states, "Where there is no vision, the people perish." Vision (in this instance) means to have a dream, a goal, and a hope! Vision deals with being able to see, imagine, or perceive. If one cannot see something better or rather see beyond one's current situation, one will soon give up hoping that things will get better. One will begin to accept his or her current circumstances as "all there is," and so, the only way out for that person becomes death. (Hence, we have the phrase "get rich or die trying!" made popular again by 50 Cent through his album and the movie of the same title.) With that being said, it is easy to understand why so many of our inner city youth act out and behave as they do!

Hopelessness (fear that things are never going to get better) leads to despair, and despair leads to suicide and murder! Whether through wild or brash outbursts of rage, sex, or drug addiction, one begins to have little to no respect for life. It becomes quite easy to take someone else's life or one's own! (Think about it!)

However

There is hope!

We must resist fear!

Fear and laziness are the enemies of success!

Fear causes doubt! Doubt causes hesitation and procrastination. This hinders us from accomplishing tasks, pursuing our dreams, and reaching our goals!

Open your eyes…Face the truth!

We must face our fears and conquer them. We will need some assistance in order to do this.

What do you fear? Why?

Recognize that you have fear. Acknowledge it (for what it is) and work to overcome it!

For God has not given us a spirit of fear, but of power and of love and of a sound mind (2 Timothy 1:7)

Fear of man will prove to be a snare, but whoever trusts in the LORD is kept safe. (Proverbs 29:25)

There is no fear in Love. But perfect love drives out fear, because fear has to do with punishment. The one who fears is not made perfect in love. (1 John 14:18)

There is one fear that every man, woman, boy, and girl should have . . .

…and that is the fear of *God!*

The fear of the LORD is the beginning of wisdom: and the knowledge of the Holy One is understanding. (Proverbs 9:10)

Guilt/
Shame

Open your eyes…Face the truth!

Guilt/Shame

In the previous chapter, we discussed *fear*—that it is the root cause of stress (pressure), depression, low self-esteem, distress, un-forgiveness and even anger. We have discussed how fear hinders us from being or becoming what we could be. Now let us discuss yet another *'fruit'* or offspring of fear that is so extremely powerful that it imprisons, nullifies and keeps a great many of us from expressing who we really are and what we really feel. Because of the overwhelming guilt and shame (which plays on our desires to be accepted and respected and also our desire to avoid being embarrassed, laughed at and ridiculed), we all hide behind a mask to cover our inadequacies and insecurities to be socially accepted. Ironically, this current generation marches under the banner, which boldly says, "Keep it real!" ("Keep it 100 %") but most will not (willingly) admit that they do not.

What is guilt?

Guilt is the nagging feeling one gets when one knows one has done something wrong. It can be the realization that something should have been said or some action taken yet was not, resulting in misfortune (some unwanted or undesired outcome). It is also the state or condition of being wrong (as in guilty of committing a crime).

What is shame?

Shame is a feeling of extreme embarrassment, disgrace, or dishonor.

Shame causes one to cringe, to shutter and to hide one's self at the very thought of some past act or experience.

Everyone feels guilty (for one thing or another)!

Some would say, "No one is innocent!"

Everyone is guilty of something!

Everyone has done or experienced something that has made them feel guilt and/or shame.

- Situation or circumstances:
  - A family member on drugs or alcohol
  - Poor living conditions (poverty)
  - Feeling that one lacks ability or knowledge that others possess
  - Failing to succeed or achieve some goal
  - Could not fulfill a promise
  - Failure to accomplish one's life dream

- Something that was not said (and now it is too late)
  - I love you
  - I'm sorry
  - I'm proud of you
  - I forgive you

- Something that was said
  - Blurting out the wrong thing at the wrong time
  - Verbally hurting a loved one's feelings

- An act such as
  - Sexual (rape, molestation, lesbian, homosexual, orgy)
  - Adultery
  - Getting caught stealing
  - Pulling a prank that hurt someone

- Not acting (to prevent harm, injury, or death)

- Someone in danger (fire, about to drink and drive, about to fall, about to use/try drugs)
- Someone in need of assistance (carrying something, is hurt, or is under attack)
- Failing to stop an argument or fight (resulting in serious injury, jail time, or death)

What's done is done (and cannot be undone).

You can never change the past (so stop trying to)!

We've got to move on! Don't dwell in the past!

Stop rehearsing the past!

Guilt and shame lead to the following:

- Depression
  - Sadness
  - Isolation—withdrawal from the world
  - Various addictions (overeating, alcohol/drugs, sexual promiscuity—variety of sexual partners)
  - Suicide

- Being unproductive (mental and or physical shutdown)

- Physical illness
  - Weakened immune system
  - Ulcers, hypertension, high blood pressure, and cancer (from anger)

- Frustration
  - Anger (yelling, cursing)
  - Bitterness (sarcasm, jealousy, slander)
  - Violence (lashing out, fighting, destroying property, murder)

Guilt/shame causes paralysis (You become mentally stuck and cannot move, like a prison for the mind.)

Guilt and/or shame can destroy your future!

Don't remain a prisoner to guilt and shame! Break free!

Admit and address guilt and shame *("Yes, I did that, but now . . .")*

What were you taught? What were you not taught?

Understand that we may have done or said some things because of what we have or have not been taught.

Our actions may have been done in ignorance, not knowing any better. Some of our actions may have been taken because the knowledge of a different or better way was not taught to us.

"Up until now, this was what I saw, so this is how I have acted."
"I didn't know any better."

One must put the past behind one's self and look forward to the future, saying,

"Yes. I did all of that, but that's not who I am now!"

Don't let anyone condemn you for past mistakes.

Don't dwell on past mistakes or let yourself (or others) label you by what you have done (or have not done).

What you can make right, make it right!
- Apologize
- Make repairs
- Buy a new one
- Start to do right

Why continue beating yourself up over something you cannot change?

Move on! Climb out! Press through!

Know yourself!

Open your eyes…Face the truth!

Identify your weaknesses and shortcomings and then work on them!

Get help! You will not be able to do this alone! Everyone needs someone to listen, to comfort and encourage them, and to let them know that they are forgiven.

Lastly, forgive yourself!

For all have sinned, and come short of the glory of God. (Romans 3:23)

Come now, and let us reason together, saith the LORD: though your sins be as scarlet, they shall be as white as snow; though they be red like crimson, they shall be as wool. (Isaiah 1:18)

If we confess our sins, he (God) is faithful and just to forgive us [our] sins, and to cleanse us from all unrighteousness. (1 John 1:9) Emphasis added

For the scripture saith, Whoever believeth on him shall not be ashamed. (Romans 10:11)

You will again have compassion on us; you will tread our sins underfoot and hurl all our iniquities into the depths of the sea. (Micah 7:19 NIV)

For God so loved the world, that he gave his only begotten son, that whosoever believeth in him should not perish, but have everlasting life. For God sent not his son into the world to condemn the world; but that the world through him might be saved. (John 3:16-17)

Self-Esteem

Open your eyes…Face the truth!

Self-Esteem
("I have worth.")

What is self-esteem?

Self-esteem is the worth one places on one's self (one's own personage). Self-esteem is how one sees one's self.

Most people (secretly) don't think very highly of themselves!

It is very important that we think highly of ourselves!

There are two types of self-esteem. One can have low self-image, or one can have high self-image (image is what one sees of one's self).

Low self-image involves the following:

- Fear of rejection. Everyone desires to be accepted, to fit in, and to belong. If one does not feel accepted, one begins to think, "I don't stack up. I'm not good enough, smart enough, etc." One may begin to alter one's self in order to gain the approval of others. If they that one desires to impress remain uninterested, then more changes will be made. When one finds that they cannot fit in and are refused acceptance, the response will manifest in the conditions listed below:

  o Depression- hopelessness
  o Sadness- down in spirit

- Indecisiveness- confused, second guessing one's self, unable to move one way or another
- Lack of confidence in one's self and in one's abilities
- Jealousy
- Talking down to or about others
- Bullying
- Thoughts of ugliness or stupidity
- Feeling of worthlessness
- Thoughts of suicide

Low self-esteem may start in the home:
- Un-nurturing and or unsupportive parents
- Parental favoritism. One child is made to feel less talented, gifted, coordinated, attractive, less loved than another sibling. (Most parents are unaware of their own actions toward their children concerning this matter.)
- Sibling rivalry. Children may develop jealousy or competition between their siblings without parental involvement or fault. One child may see his/her sibling(s) as more talented or as getting more (especially if siblings are close in age or if one needs more attention and affection).

Some sure signs are as follows:

- Teasing/bullying
- Theft
- Destruction of property
- Hostility/violence

One's home life might be quite well yet the individual may experience teasing or ridicule in school, at the playground or on the block. Thus, one's self-esteem suffers damage.

Low self-esteem will keep you from reaching your full potential!

Low self-esteem:

- Causes lack of self-confidence

- Keeps one from experiencing true happiness
- May cause one to use drugs/alcohol
- May cause one to cling to others for strength or worth (even in abusive relationships)
- May cause one to think that giving themselves sexually will make people love him/her
- May cause one not to care for his/her appearance (having poor hygiene)
- May cause one to go to extremes in order to get attention (acting wild, becoming overbearing)
- May cause one to dress in a certain way to draw attention to one's self (wearing very little or clothes that are too revealing), or one might cover up, hoping to hide within and behind oversized dark clothing
- May cause one to tear down someone else to make one's self feel good (hiding their own pain, awkwardness, and unhappiness)

Don't ever think that you have high self-esteem if you have a habit of tearing down others!

Factors for low self-esteem:

- One's socio-economic status compared to what others may have
- Lack of education, opportunities and nurturing
- Physical and verbal abuse

High or healthy self-esteem:

- Says, "I'm cool with me! I'm not perfect—but I'm good."
- Doesn't have to tear anyone down to make one's self feel or look good
- Doesn't have to prove one's talents, abilities or worth to anyone in
- order to be validated
- Is freedom from the following:
    o Addictions
    o Stereotypes
    o Trends, etc.

- Makes decisions and moves for the better, striving for higher goals!

- Doesn't allow drugs, gangs, abuse, neglect or negative influences to stop them (despite color, age, background or education, etc.)
- Enables one to follow his/her own course and not the crowd

Factors for high self-esteem or healthy self-image:

- Knowing one's self (being honest, doing self-inventory)
- Not taking one's self too seriously
- Learning to appreciate one's strengths and weaknesses
- Refusing to accept things that are not going to build one's self up
- Working on one's self (spirit/mind and body)! Success takes work. (Maintaining high self-esteem takes work.)

The ugliest people in the world are those who have "stank" attitudes! They are never satisfied and are always bored. They dislike everything, hate almost everyone. (That's low self-esteem.) They act in this manner to hide their own insecurities and self-hate (pity).

We have far more worth than people will ever tell us! Realize this fact, embrace it and press on toward greatness!

Healthy self-esteem greatly determines how far or high one will go in life! Aim high!

High self-esteem is rare and uncommon!

More on self-esteem
(Some things to remember)

We are created in God's image and in his likeness! (We were made with His qualities and also we were made to function as He functions (on an infinitely smaller scale)!

Whatever you think of yourself in your heart, that's what you are or shall become. Make sure that what you think (meditate on) is positive!

Even your name has meaning and a purpose! Find out what it means and live up to it! If your name is made up, then make up a meaning for it and live up to it!

Every time someone calls your name, they are actually speaking or confirming what you were destined to become. However, because most of us haven't the slightest idea what our name means, we drift around, not knowing who we truly are. After all, when asked who we are, we reply, "I'm (your name goes here)." If your name means "fool" (for instance), then that is who you are. Many of us will make up a name or turn to the streets to give us our identity (which is usually the exact opposite of what we were meant to be. Ironically, we do our very best to live up to that name. Sometimes this is good, but more often than not, this is not the case.)

A blind man knows he cannot see—but those who *live in darkness* (ignorance), don't realize that they are blind! (Get wisdom, get understanding!)

Finally

In everything that you do or say, pursue, claim and conduct yourself with excellence!

And God said, <u>Let us make man in our image, after our likeness</u>: and let them have dominion over the fish of the sea, and over the fowl of the air, and over the cattle, and over every creeping thing that creepeth upon the earth. <u>So God created man in his own image, in the image of God created he him; male and female created he them</u>. (Genesis 1:26, 27)

I will praise thee; for <u>I am fearfully and wonderfully made</u>: marvelous are thy works; and that my soul knoweth right well. (Psalm 139:14)

And to all those who put their trust in the Lord Jesus Christ…

Beloved, now we are the children of God, and what we will be has not yet been revealed. We know that when He appears, we will be like Him, for we will see Him as He is. (1 John 3:2—Berean Literal Bible)

I. L. Jackson

Peer Pressure

Open your eyes…Face the truth!

Peer Pressure
(Follow the leader!)

What do you think is most important to a teenager? Is it clothes? Is it money? Is it to please his/her parents?

A teen's most important desire is to be socially accepted by his or her peers (it may be nearly as important for adults). With that in mind, we can begin to understand why appearance, clothes and even parties become a teen's preoccupation.

The teenager of today is under so much pressure. Society or what has been socially acceptable, has convinced our youth that without the latest: clothes, sneakers and boots, bags, hats, iPods, portable PlayStations, cell phones, etc., they are not cool! Some wouldn't be caught dead wearing last year's gear!

The influence of what we (and our youths) see on TV and in movies; hear on the radio, see or read on social media—of corruption, gangs, violence, drug and gun dealers, sex and prostitution have become major factors in the shaping of our lives. In fact, peer pressure is so powerful in the lives of teens that it will cause those that have never given any problems to their parents to rebel against authority, reject what they have been taught, how they were raised and their beliefs. In turn, they may embrace and practice negative behaviors!

What is peer pressure?

It is the pressure felt by us from someone of similar circumstances to behave or think and act in a certain way.

It is the influence of others of the same peer group (age, race, economic status, or current situation) urging us to act or think a certain way because they are doing it.

Trends and fads are examples of peer pressure!

- Peer pressure plays on or against our individuality!
- Peer pressure persuades us (through our lack of self-esteem and insecurities) to clone (act, dress and talk like) others or those who are in the majority

We must wear a certain kind of jeans, boots, shoes/sneakers, shirt, etc. All of these must be the current brand name (that is in style at this very moment) in order to be accepted, to feel and be considered cool.

Peer pressure plays on our desires and also our lusts!
We all want the following:

Attention—to be noticed, found attractive
- Acceptance—we want friends, we desire to be loved, we crave for some companions and to belong to something
- To feel good about ourselves

Many of us look to others and how they perceive us as a gauge for how we think of ourselves. This should not be!

The need to be popular, for example, will cause a person who has low self-esteem to do foolish things in order to boost their egos, feel accepted and get attention.

Peer pressure will cause a person with low self-esteem to do the following:

- Steal/rob
- Act violently (bully others to make one's self feel powerful, cut or harm one's self)

Open your eyes…Face the truth!

- Have a baby to feel loved and accepted
- Become a vandal (seeking fame, notoriety, and attention)
- Use drugs/alcohol (to overcome shyness; to cope with stress, abuse, neglect, grief from a loss, loneliness; and to fit in)

Many of us will do whatever it takes to become popular!

Peer pressure and addiction are closely linked. One may fall into addiction from being pressured into performing, using (whatever) for the first time. (For many individuals, one time is all it takes!)

- *"I dare you . . ."*
- *"Bet you can't . . ."*
- *"Let's try some of this—mixed with . . ."*

(These phrases may be the most deadly propositions one can make concerning peer pressure.)

Negative peer pressure enslaves a person by playing on his/her insecurities and the desire to be accepted.

Negative peer pressure causes one to act against good or moral judgment!

Scenario

A sober person is skeptical about getting into a car filled with people who have been drinking. The driver is clearly drunk. The driver says, *"Come on chicken, a little beer can't hurt my driving!"* The other passengers rally behind the driver saying, *"Come on!"* The sober person eventually gives in to the peer pressure. They crash and everyone in the car dies—but the driver. (This happens far too often!)

It takes a strong person with a healthy self-image and confidence to resist the influence of (negative) peer pressure.

Resisting negative peer pressure may cause the following:

- One to be left out of many gatherings and events
- One to lose some close friends and associates
- One to lose popularity because he/she refuses to go along with the crowd
- One to be talked about or shunned to some degree because of his/her stance
- One may find that he/she has become the object of bullying

Resisting negative peer pressure shows great strength of character and although it may cost us friends, popularity, etc., at first, it brings great rewards at the end!

- Not being addicted to drugs/alcohol
- Not ending up in jail
- Being free from sexually transmitted diseases (such as genital warts, syphilis and AIDS)
- Not paying fines or having to do community service because you were caught committing vandalism

Think about this:

How many fights and violent acts could be avoided if there was no negative peer pressure from our friends? How many times have we seen (or experienced) two or more people involved in a conflict over something that may be quite small—yet the situation explodes into a violent fight? In many cases, these "fires" were ignited or fueled by instigators (those who urge i.e. pressure—and keep the situation hot!) Consequently, those who were involved in the original dispute wind up: getting into trouble, being injured (or worse); and perhaps others who have become involved. Increasingly, small conflicts are ending in death! (And those who are dying are our inner city youth!)

See how dangerous the effect of negative peer pressure has become? This generation would rather kill or be killed just so they can look good and be accepted by their peers. They would rather join in the fight (ride or bang with their friends) than to stop it! What ever happened to the pursuit of love, peace, and happiness?

Open your eyes…Face the truth!

When we give in to peer-pressure, we are allowing others to control us. We give them power over us! In turn, these persons tell us how to act, how and what to think. We know better—yet we still do something—stupid!

We compromise the following:

- Our position—where we stand in our hearts, our integrity
- Our opinion—what we think
- Our morals—what we know and hold to be good and what is bad
- Our beliefs—what we understand and hold fast to
- Our upbringing—what we have been taught

Peer pressure comes from the following:

- Personal relationships (family and friends)
- Social media, TV, radio, movies, magazines, billboards, etc.
- Environments or surroundings (ghettos, suburbs, projects)
- Parental favoritism—one child may feel pressure to do as follows:
  - Overachieve
  - Act like a sister/brother, losing his/her own identity
  - Try too hard
  - Act out (attempting to receive attention)
  - Ignore, downplay his/her own gifts and talents

Sometimes, parents expect one child to share the same gifts and talents that another sibling may excel at or wish for one child to act as another. This does great harm to the self-esteem/image of the child who tries to live up to the standard that was placed on them by his/her parents. The child may grow hateful toward his/her brother or sister and resentful toward his/her parents. Personal relationships (family and friends) may suffer because unresolved bitterness is often carried into adulthood.

Parents, all of us, must recognize and learn to appreciate the individual gifts, talents, personalities and beauty of our children; and then we must work to nurture, support and guide them in the way that they *should* go!

A ticking bomb is created by parents who constantly ask one child, *"Why can't you be like . . . ?"* The hate and jealousy created by pitting one sibling against another may last well into their adulthood, potentially ripping the family apart!

Peer pressure is a tool used in the following:

- Advertisements ("Everyone has this. What? You don't have this?")
- Political circles ("We're voting this way, all of the others are!")
- Social circles ("Anyone who's anyone goes here, does this!")
- The food, car, clothing and beverage industries *("You've got to have or try our product.")*

We are all special and unique! No one can do what you do like you do it!

We must become comfortable with who we are and not be overly concerned with the abilities of others!

We must find out what we are good at and work to excel at those things in our own way!

Having confidence in one's self and one's abilities helps us to stand against (negative) peer pressure. We will not be easily moved by the persistent urging of others to do things that are not good for us!

Positive Peer Pressure

Peer pressure can be positive or negative!

I know that we have spent a lot of time discussing negative peer pressure; however, peer pressure is not always bad. There is such a thing as positive peer pressure. Just as negative peer pressure often brings negative results; positive peer pressure brings about positive endings!

Positive pressure from family and friends encourages us to do the following:

Open your eyes…Face the truth!

- Strive to achieve higher goals
- Stay away from harmful drugs/alcohol
- Save sex until marriage
- Be honest, not to cheat or to steal
- Abstain from violence

On the other hand

Constant pressures to have what others have and to do as others do tend to cause the following:
- Jealousy and envy (resentment)
- Debt
- Disappointments
- Theft/robberies
- Violence
- Murder!

Change your mind! Refuse to be sucked into negative peer pressure!

Once again, having confidence in one's self and one's abilities helps us to stand against (negative) peer pressure. We will not be easily moved by the persistent urging of others to do things that are not good for us!

Consider this:

If we—you or I—are going to spend all of our time trying to be (like) someone else, then who is going to be you? Who is going to be—me?

My son, if sinners entice you, do no consent. If they say, "Come with us, Let us lie in wait for blood, Let us ambush the innocent without cause; Let us swallow them alive like Sheol, Even whole as those who go down to the pit; We will find all kinds of precious wealth, we will fill our houses with spoil; Throw in your lot with us, We shall have one purse," My son, do not walk in the way with them Keep your feet from their path, (Proverbs 1:10-15)

He who walks with the wise men will be wise, But the companion of fools will suffer harm. (Proverbs 13:20)

A man of too many friends comes to ruin, But there is a friend who sticks closer than a brother. (Proverbs 18:24)

Do not participate in the unfruitful deeds of darkness, but instead even expose them; (Ephesians 5:11)

<u>And do not be conformed to this world, but be ye transformed by the renewing of your mind</u>, so that you may prove what the will of God is, that which is good and acceptable and perfect. (Romans 12:2)

Open your eyes…Face the truth!

Diversity

38

Diversity

What is diversity?

Diversity can be said to be the state or condition of having many differences within the same kind, species or classification. (Like looking at a garden and seeing that within this garden there is a *diversity* of plants and flowers, varying in size, shape and color.

What does it mean to be diverse?

Diverse means numerous differences (variations in size, shape, color, texture, width, density, etc.).

In nature, no two things are exactly alike.

It is man that has created uniformity, duplication, mass production and (dare I say)—cloning.

Mankind has a preoccupation with sameness or alikeness.

In itself, uniformity does not seem to raise any major concern—yet alikeness becomes a concern when it is taken to the extreme and forced upon others.

When the idea of uniformity goes too far, the results are as follows:

- Racism—the belief that everyone should be the same color, that one's own race is or should dominate; that other races should serve and be treated as inferior
- Copycats—people who lack originality of thought, losing their own identity in pursuit of being like someone else (acting and talking like that person, doing the same things that he/she does, wearing the same clothes and hairstyle and so on)
- Clones—the idea, belief or practice of isolating certain traits (genetic patterns) and duplicating them over and over and over again (like taking a great warriors' genes and creating a vast army of super soldiers that are exactly like him in every way)!
- Conflicts, dissension, and rebellion—some are bound to rebel! Some will refuse to give up their individuality. This will cause tensions, outbreaks, separations and even wars!

Unity and uniformity are not exactly the same.

Unity refers to individuals who have a common interest and who have the same mind-set, coming together to fulfill a purpose. Using music as an example; voices that are singing in "unity"—sound similar. They are singing in the same key. Even though this may sound ok for a short time, it isn't until the voices break up that the song begins to soar! This is called harmony! Harmony is varying voices or sounds blending together to create one melody. Each voice, though it differs from others (some higher and others lower), holds its own note or position yet lends itself to the 'unity' of the song. The result is a beautiful melody!

Once again, uniformity or unison can be described as every voice singing in the same exact pitch (octave, level or tone). Though the song may sound OK for a minute, there is a flatness or noticeable lack of something (over time)!

Let us be ever mindful of both the pros and cons of uniformity because if all things were to become the same (or having the same function), life itself would lose its excitement; innovation and progress would cease. Only one thing would be accomplished—and that, to the point of being overly developed! Everything else would be neglected, decay, fall apart and die.

Uniformity has its place—but diversity adds *zest* to life!

What's your favorite ice cream, your favorite food, song or TV show?

What if:

- *There was only one flavor of ice cream?*
- *There was only one thing to eat in the whole world, and there was only one way it was prepared?*
- *There was only one TV show or song and it was played twenty-four hours a day, seven days a week?*
- *Everything (trees, mountains, cars, chairs, houses, buildings, etc.) were the same shade of gray or brown?*
- *It rained all day every day, and each day looked exactly like the day before?*

Just imagine!

What if everyone looked exactly alike—every man the same height and weight, the same complexion, eye color, hairstyle and tone of voice? Moreover, what if everyone had the exact same personality, even the same way of thinking? Imagine that every woman and child were the same as well!

What if:
- There was only night and no day?
- Everyone did the same job?
- Everyone had the same exact talent (singing, dancing, playing basketball)?

Diversity is necessary!

Diversity is beautiful!

Look at the human body. If all of our body parts were eyes, then how could we talk, walk or hear? If every part were the spleen or intestines, we would have no hands, no heart and no brain.

Open your eyes...Face the truth!

Many different parts make up the human body! These parts function according to how they were made. Our body parts work in harmony toward a common goal. That goal is to keep you and me alive and as healthy as possible!

We need diversity!

If all of us and all things were exactly the same, the world would be bland, boring and most likely, empty. We would probably go crazy because of the monotony! One person might say to him/herself, *"I'm going to grow a beard,"* or *"I'm going to dye my hair,"* only to find as he/she walks outside that he or she still looks like everyone else because everyone thinks exactly the same!

It is the insane individual that desires everyone to be exactly the same!

If such a person were to get his or her way, sooner or later, someone would rise up, stating that everyone should be something else. Then that (first) person might find that he/she fails to fit the new mold!

Some may take offense at these observations:

- **Without Europeans** (Caucasians or white people), African Americans (black people) would not seek to straighten, lengthen, or dye their hair. We would not have such things as Italian food (from Italy) for instance, hamburgers (from Germany), fine cuisine and assorted pastries (from France).
- **Without Africans and African Americans**, Caucasians (white people) would not pursue suntans (bronze or darker skin), they would not braid their hair nor would they seek thicker, fuller lips. Such things as prints on shirts and other clothing, the cell phone, the traffic light, the clock, ice cream, the heating furnace, the air conditioner, the refrigerator and blood banks, rock and roll, jazz, the blues, soul, R & B, and hip-hop music (as well as the culture) would not exist. We would not have the pyramids or any of the other races for that matter, for the remains of the earliest existence of man was found in Africa! Some may not like this next statement; however, it is interesting to note that studies show that every (other) race originated from Africans.
- **Without Orientals** (Chinese, Japanese, Koreans, West Indians, etc.), we would not know how to make silk. The world would be without

ceramic china plates and dishes, beautiful vases, tapestries and rugs, various kinds of paper, India ink, gun powder (uh . . . maybe I shouldn't have mentioned that one), fireworks, all types of spices, and foods. The most well-known of the martial arts, certain lovable breeds of dogs, some of the best cars (Honda, Acura, Toyota, Lexus), anime, many popular hairstyles, sumi-e brush paintings and calligraphy, origami (paper art), advances in technology (video games and game systems, radio, TV, computers and robotics), also many of our favorite toys would not exist.

- **The Native Americans** (Mexicans, Incas, Peruvians and all of those great many cultures that I confess I am ignorant of) all have contributed greatly to the life and lifestyles that we now take for granted.

No race or culture is better than another. Each race or culture has great value and brings something wonderful to this world—and to this life!

We must learn to embrace diversity!

Imagine what life would be like and what could be accomplished if you and all of your friends, classmates or coworkers and family members were to forget all of your petty differences, come up with a goal, formulate a plan to work toward it and carry out that plan. After that goal was met, a new goal would be set and so on!

If everyone suddenly forgot their prejudices and began to work together to reach that goal, there would be nothing that could stop us!

We must learn to appreciate diversity and we must also learn from diversity!

- *Without death, how could we appreciate the value of life and what life offers?*
- *Without evil people, what would make us strive or seek out what is good?*
- *Without the darkness of night, how could we then appreciate the beauty and brightness of day?* (Night has its own beauty too!)

- Even the four seasons bring something unique and wonderful as they come and go during their never-ending cycle. Notice, each time they come around, they are not quite the same as they were the year before!

Diversity is "all that!" It's "what's poppin'!"--" It's what's "good!" It "bangs!" It "rocks" etc.!

We have diverse likes, dislikes, talents, skin color, eye color, hair color and texture, heights, weights (body structures) just as the trees, flowers, plants, fruit, animals, fish, birds, mountains, streams, rivers, lakes, and oceans all differ from each other!

Everything and everyone have their own unique beauty!
How do you differ from your friends or coworkers?

Do you see your uniqueness as a good thing or bad? Why?

What special quality do you have that sets you apart from your peers?

Can that quality be improved if so, how?

There is one thing in which we should not differ; that is, in our love and kindness toward one another.

Have all not all one father? Hath not one God created us? Why do we deal treacherously every man against his brother, by profaning the covenant of our fathers? (Malachi 2:10)

My brethren, have not the faith of our Lord Jesus Christ, [the Lord] of glory, with respect of persons. (James 2:1)

After this I beheld, and, lo, a great multitude, which no man could number, of all nations, and kindreds, and people, and tongues, stood before the throne, and before the Lamb, clothed with white robes, and palms in their hands; (Revelation 7:9)

Slave

It is horrible to think that in these days and times, the cruelty, the inhumanity, the wearisome drudgery, and terrible condition of slavery still exists. What is more shameful and frightening than realizing that slavery still exists is the fact that many walk throughout life unaware they are in bondage.

What is a slave?

A slave is someone who is owned and controlled and is the servant of another.

We all are slaves to someone or something!

Who or what has mastery over you?

Who or what is it that calls to you and you have no choice but to respond?

Did you know that whoever or whatever you serve (with your body), that person or thing is your master?

- Food (Overeating)
- Drugs/alcohol
- Sex/pornography
- Anger (violence, rage)
- Depression (hopelessness)

- Fear/anxiety/phobias
- Certain friends (girlfriend, boyfriend, peer pressure)
- Guilt/shame
- (Receiving) Attention, accolades
- Power (craving control)
- Job/business (workaholic)
- Church (neglecting home and or family)
- Fashion (have to have the latest, following trends and fads)
- Shopping (shopaholic)
- Television
- Video games, etc.
- A way of thinking (as a race or culture).

Get a hold of "The Willie Lynch Letter" (and read it thoroughly) because it gives specific instructions on how to break the will of an individual as well as an entire group of people, how to control them, and how to keep them mentally enslaved for hundreds of years!

I will not go into detail at this time. The letter explains itself. It is not my desire to speak about racial issues or incite anyone to anger. However, I mentioned the reading of the letter in order to support my point—that we can be enslaved to a way of thinking that causes us to act in a self-destructive manner. (I do mention some of the effects of this letter in the chapter dealing with "The Need and Purpose of Fathers.")

*("The Willie Lynch Letter" can be found on the Internet or in book form, The Willie Lynch Letter and the Making of a Slave, published by Lushena Books.)

I also suggest reading about Adolf Hitler, Charles Manson, David Koresh and other such men who were able to manipulate and control others into doing their will.

If there is someone or something that has control over you (what you think, how you act, where you go, when and what you eat, what you wear, etc.), then you are enslaved, and whatsoever it may be that has control over you is you master!

Open your eyes…Face the truth!

Break free!

Scenario:

Imagine that you have been thrust into solitary confinement in a maximum-security prison and that you can no longer remember how long you have been there. Suddenly, all of the doors open, your shackles fall off, the guard have disappeared, the gate opens, and you receive a word that the warden has given you a full pardon! You might think, "Great! I'm free! I'm no longer a prisoner!" That may be correct; however, although you have been set free, you have yet to take advantage of your newly granted liberty. Until you get up and walk out of the place where you were confined, you shall remain imprisoned though you are no longer a prisoner!

This is the case for many of us! We have heard the truth about our situations, and the knowledge of that truth has given us the power to change our lives, yet we do not believe that we are free! We have been trained to accept our current condition. We have become comfortable where we are; we have been deceived into believing that we cannot make it and that we ourselves or our situations cannot change. We believe that it's too hard, it's too uncomfortable, and we fear that we shall fail. (Remember our discussion on fear?)

We all fail from time to time. Failure brings humility and an appreciation of success once it is achieved! If we never experienced failing, we would become arrogant; our heads would rival the Goodyear blimp in size.

Do you wish to remain a slave? If your answer is no, then how badly do you wish to be free?

One of the greatest examples of a person, who was a slave yet refused to accept her condition and eventually obtained her freedom (through much courage and determination), was the late Harriet Tubman. Harriet was born into slavery. She was snatched from her family at a very young age and sold to another family. Harriet slept on the floor with the dogs and ate the same things that the dogs ate. As a little girl, she suffered much abuse and was forced to serve her masters even though she was sickly for some time. (But all of this served to prepare Harriet for what she would accomplish when she became an

48

adult.) Although she had gone through great suffering as a slave, Ms. Tubman was not content to remain in that state. Indignation (an anger fueled by the injustices she saw and experienced) rose from within her, burning like a great fire! That fire raged higher and hotter and became so strong that it moved her to take action! That action came to be known as the Underground Railroad, a movement led by Ms. Tubman (who received aid from courageous whites who hid Harriet and her companions in their homes at different points along their journey), which helped hundreds of African Americans to obtain their freedom.

Through one woman's courageous actions and self-determination, many others were able to escape slavery! Ms. Tubman not only gained her freedom, she was able to keep it until the day she died! That is a great accomplishment! (I encourage you to read about Ms. Tubman and many of the other freedom fighters throughout history when you get a chance.) It only takes one determined individual to start a movement.

Freedom (once it is gained) is not (so) easily kept!

One who has gained his or her freedom must learn to maintain it, or he or she may slip and become enslaved again. (A recaptured slave received punishment [whipped, tortured]; he or she was watched more closely, was treated with increased harshness, and was guarded all the more to discourage any future attempts to escape.) One, who escaped enslavement, if recaptured, suffered and found one's self in worse conditions (being recaptured) than he or she was before the escape attempt. The likelihood of that person regaining his or her freedom again was very slim.

We have been discussing slavery in terms of one person or group of persons oppressing another group; however, it is the same for anyone who may be enslaved to an addiction as we have mentioned earlier in this chapter. If one gains freedom from addiction, one must be very careful not to entertain any of the things that caused him or her to fall into addiction in the first place. If one falls again (has a relapse), it may be harder to escape (at present) than it was the first time. One may find him or herself in a struggle for many years, trying to regain the freedom he or she once enjoyed. (This is a sad truth that happens daily for many people.)

Let's look at some addictions (again):

Open your eyes…Face the truth!

- Food (Overeating)
- Drugs/alcohol
- Sex/pornography
- Anger (violence, rage)
- Depression (hopelessness)
- Fear/anxiety/phobias
- Certain friends (girlfriend, boyfriend, peer pressure)
- Guilt/shame
- (Receiving) Attention through pity (being a professional victim), through accolades (praise for some ability or personal quality)
- Power (craving control)
- Job/business (workaholic)
- Church work (neglecting home and family to do the will of the pastor and to take care for his needs and projects)
- Fashion (have to have the latest, following trends and fads)
- Shopping (shopaholic)
- Television
- Video games, etc.
- Social Media

How did Harriet Tubman accomplish such a feat?

How was she able to maintain her freedom and help others to obtain it for themselves?

1. She did not accept what was told to her about herself (i.e. *"slave"*, *"you ain't nothin'"*, *"nigger'"*, etc.). She knew she was better and worth far more than what other people were telling her.
2. She gained as much knowledge as she could (about what she wanted to do) in order to help her accomplish her goal.
3. She took a certain path while obtaining her own freedom and did not deviate from that path even while freeing others (certain places she would not go, certain people she would not take along like cowards, complainers, those who couldn't follow directions or take orders, those whose minds were not made up). Why did she take some and not others? She did not want to lose her freedom!

4. She was willing to die for freedom! In order to gain freedom, something must die (old ways of thinking, habits, certain friendships, etc.).

5. Harriet did not think of herself as a slave. Her thoughts were *"I am free!"* (Many, who have been set free from addiction, have been told that they will always be recovering, and so they always have a mind-set that tells them, *"One day I will fall again."* But Ms. Tubman teaches us that once you have been freed, you must have the mind-set that reminds you, *"I'm not going back. I'd rather die first!"* That is the determination of someone who truly values freedom!

In truth, many of us have not grown to hate those things (addictions or whatever) that have enslaved us enough to adopt the "do or die" mind-set. We still like (even love) those things (or people) that have enslaved us; therefore, there is no true change (although we try)! That is why we continue to return to them (no matter how badly we are treated). If we did not (still) like them, we would not want to be around them. However, we have fond memories of fun times, of partying, and so on! We hold on to those (cherished) memories (which are the very things that keep us going back), hoping that those good times and feelings will be returned to us, but they seldom do. In order to break free from whatever it is that has enslaved us, we must hate it! We must hate the fact that it has power over us, and we must desire with everything in us to break free from that person's or thing's control. If we do not come to that point, we will remain a slave and may perhaps be killed by the thing that has enslaved us!

Think about it.

We don't do the following with those people and things that we 'dislike'. We don't:
- Interact with
- Entertain
- Hang around or visit
- Have conversations with them; we have no rap!

What you think and believe you are—that is what you shall become!

You are more than what others tell you! You are not stupid or less than anyone else; you can learn (you may just have another learning style than others); you can get off of the drugs (and never go back); you can quit smoking, drinking, whatever; and you can conquer your addiction(s); change your habits, and your life! (There is one who can help!)

You are not what you have been labeled (you do not have to remain under that label)!

We are all priceless!

The drug addict, the prostitute, the homeless man or woman—all of these have worth! We look down at them and fault them for their mistakes yet seek mercy and understanding when we make our own. We are so heartless, selfish, and uncaring toward our fellow man. (Lord, help us! Help me!)

We all have boundless potential!

This world and many of its people don't want you to know this. Our imaginations and hope are being stolen! We see through frustrated eyes through pain, abuse and neglect. These are the things, which enslave us and hinder us from seeing the possibilities all around us. Proverbs 29:18 of the Bible states, *"Where there is no vision (hope, goal, imagination), the people perish."*

Gain your freedom! (No matter where you are in this life!)

Stay free!

Obtaining your freedom may cost you all that you currently have. You may lose everything that you thought mattered (that you cared about), even those you once cared for and loved!

Are you the One? (I'm a fan of The Matrix. What can I say?)

Do you believe that you are a slave or are you free?

Are you willing to do what must be done to gain your freedom and then to keep it? (Freedom is not easily won, and it is difficult, at times, to maintain!)

The enslavement that I have been speaking of is that of the mind—it is a prison without walls, floor, ceiling, windows, or doors. It is an enslavement that is not always visible yet is very real! It is from this prison that we must escape, from which we must gain our freedom.

Free your mind!
(There is a way!)

The Spirit of the LORD [is] upon me, because he hath anointed me to preach the gospel to the poor; he hath sent me to heal the brokenhearted, to preach deliverance to the captives, and recovering of sight to the blind, to set at liberty them that are bruised. (Luke 4:18)

Therefore do not let sin reign in your mortal body so that you obey its lusts, (Romans 6:12)

For sin shall not be master over you, for you are not under the law but under grace. (Romans6:14)

Do you not know that to whom you yield yourselves as slaves for obedience, you are slaves to him whom you obey, whether of sin to death, or of obedience to righteousness (Romans 6:16—Berean Literal Bible)

For we also once were foolish ourselves, disobedient, deceived, enslaved to various lusts and pleasures, spending our life in malice and envy, hateful, and hating one another. (Titus 3:3)

Open your eyes…Face the truth!

Just keeping it real!

You must be buggin' if you think I'm doing drugs.
Did you hit your head on something?
Test me. I'm not fraudin'.
And I'm not drinking any alcohol to hang with y'all.
I have too many dreams and goals to let drugs take control of my mind, body
and soul.
Don't stop me—I'm on a roll!
See drugs make your liver and brain swell and kills brain-cells, kid.
I won't do 'em, I won't sell 'em! A drug dealer's a killer!
I can say it no realer—and you can bet I won't smoke cigarettes.
"No!" is my answer. Cigarettes cause Cancer--hurting my teeth and gums…
…getting smoke all in my lungs!
No thanks! I don't want it!
I'll be the one who's never done it…
And still—I remain one of the coolest you've ever hung with!

Written by: I. L. Jackson

Drugs/Alcohol

Open your eyes…Face the truth!

Drugs/Alcohol
(The Gateway)

With all of the negative experiences one encounters throughout one's life—abuse, neglect, various frustrations, rejections, hardships, loss of family/loved ones and such—the use of drugs (both illegal and legal) have become a convenient way out for many who feel that they can no longer cope without their assistance. Such persons have fallen into the pit of hopelessness and despair, thinking that drugs/alcohol will help them to cope, to forget their problems, and to feel better. This is particularly the case for many who live in the inner cities, yet the appeal of drugs and alcohol has reached to the suburbs and into the more rural areas. In fact, alcohol abuse is nothing new to any area! Through their usage and sales, people are becoming convinced that drugs are the only solution to relieve the pain of their current condition. In reality, drugs are a snare and a trap for both the user and dealer! Drugs have a two-pronged attack whose results are deadly!

- The first trap is drugs' addictive attributes. We can liken this to a bear trap that springs shut on its user when the user least suspects it. One's very first hit may be the start of a lifelong roller coaster ride of misery, troubles and eventually death.
- The second deadly attribute of drugs is that it accelerates destructive behavior. Drugs are indeed a gateway leading one (very quickly) down a path of destruction and eventually death!

Drug effects extend to one's family, friends, job or business, and environment. Without help, death is inevitable!

What are drugs?

A drug is a substance (not food) that alters the way the mind and or body functions.

- Perception—what one sees (distance or closeness of things looked at or thought of)
- Feelings/mood—stimulated (energized, motivated), depressed (slowed down, mellow, drowsy)

(Illegal) Drugs distort reality and trick the mind or body into feeling or acting in a certain way!

All drugs are dangerous; some are helpful (in small doses) while others are truly harmful. (Illegal) drugs have harmful, long-term side effects!

- Diarrhea
- Lung and heart trouble
- Circulatory problems
- Cancer
    o Mouth/gums/throat
    o Lungs
    o Kidneys
    o Liver, etc.

- Brain cell as well as other cell damage, affecting the following:
    o Memory
    o Morals/judgment
    o Inhibitions
    o Restraint /self-control
    o Alertness/awareness
    o Natural body functions/movement

(Illegal) Drugs feed the mind and body false information!

- Feeling of warmth (when it's actually cold)
- Power/strength
- Hallucinations
- Changes perception—the unattractive becomes attractive, things that are very near look farther away than they really are
- Gives false courage

The link between mind and body becomes stunted!

- Reaction times
- Movement in general may become delayed or hindered completely as with GHB (liquid ecstasy)

- One may experience breathing problems
- May fall into a coma or even die

When the mind is weakened, it loses its defenses and becomes open to the stimuli around it. The mind becomes more accepting of the thoughts that enter it.

To put it into clearer terms, the mind releases its' restraints and inhibitions!

- If one is angry inside, that anger will manifest physically
- If one is perverse (in one's heart), then sex and perversion will be acted out
- If one is violent, then violence will result

There is an old saying, *"A drunken man speaks a sober man's mind."* This means that drugs/alcohol causes the user to speak what he or she is really thinking.

Also (in the same manner):

What is spoken to a person may be acted out:

- A girl or woman may be coaxed into performing a sexual act or perhaps she's so drugged up that she doesn't know what is happening to her.
- One might take a dangerous dare and become seriously injured or killed.
- One may act out on any wild suggestion, causing great shame and or embarrassment when one finally comes to one's senses.

One may be persuaded to commit acts of vandalism, sex, robbery, assault, even murder!

One definition of *"blunt"* (the term used for the brand of cigar whose paper is smoked with marijuana) is a *"dull object"* or *"to make dull."* Dull as in *"dullard"*—which means unintelligent (stupid)!

Under the influence of drugs, many (intelligent) individuals make stupid and costly decisions.

What the mind once fought against, hid from, hid away—or refused to accept becomes more attractive and more acceptable.

One who has low self-esteem, who is depressed or who is overwhelmed with problems can now be persuaded into committing suicide by one's own thoughts. (But are they really one's own thoughts?)

The thought will come to a drugged and depressed person, saying, *"Just end it all! You're ugly, clumsy, overweight, stupid, a failure* (or a combination of things); *you can't do anything right. Nobody cares about you anyway!"*

This is a lie told to you by the *"spirit"* that has entered the individual through drugs!

The spirit may be one that was present (with this person) all along but now has gained power or control of the person's mind, which has taken the drug. The person's mental defenses have been weakened and this negative thought or spirit has been set free to grow and pressure this person to act out *its* will.

Drugs and alcohol trap and enslave the user! One can consider one's self very fortunate if he/she has tried drugs and have not become ensnared!

Drugs pit the mind and the body at odds with each other!

Without the mind working correctly, the body begins to malfunction.

(Example: Certain drugs, like cocaine, cause the heart to beat faster yet the body is told by the mind, *"Chill—all is well."* This may cause one to have heart attack or stroke because the heart is given the message that more blood is needed, the body is in action, yet the body is at rest. This is a great malfunction.) If the mind and body continue to work against each other, the result will be a breakdown and possibly death.

Open your eyes…Face the truth!

There are some, who try drugs (for the first time) and never use them again. And then there are some that have tried drugs and will never do anything again!

Many have died from extensive drug usage; some will die the very first time they use! Don't gamble with your life. You may be the unfortunate one.

Your next hit may be the one that takes you out of here!

Prolonged drug/alcohol use:

- Causes brain damage—destroys brain cells (which control speech, memory, and certain movements)
- Damages the lungs and throat—mouth cancer (gum, tongue, and throat)
- Causes circulatory problems—shrinking of the veins, thus making the heart pumps at a faster rate
- Damages the heart, kidney, and liver—drugs/alcohol poison and pollute these organs, bore holes, and make them function improperly, if at all

Drugs/alcohol eats you away from the inside out! (Illegal) drugs begin to destroy the body from the very first contact!

That which (illegal) drugs destroy cannot be regenerated or restored to its original state!

Note: To mention the names of the various drugs at this point is unimportant. Let the doctors and pharmacists explain the names and their effects. (A child finds a gun and dies while playing with it. Who cares what the name of the gun was or the caliber of the bullet. A child is dead and there's nothing anyone can do to bring the child back. The gun could have been named "Pookie".)

The questions that should be asked are:

- This child was not trained or taught that he or she should never touch guns. *Why?*
- How was the gun obtained?

- Who left the gun in a place where the child could find it?

(Let us return to our original thought.)

How were the drugs obtained?

Were there any traumatic events that may have triggered the initial drug usage?

What was the home and surrounding environment like? (Was there any drugs or abuse present?)

Why was this person not taught about the dangers of drug use?

Why do people start to use drugs?

- Peer pressure—to fit in or be considered cool
- To cope with stress
- Hide one's insecurities (fears or feelings of awkwardness)
- Curiosity—"I'll try anything once"
- We see our parents or relative using it
- To fight grief or depression from the following:

  o Loss of family member or friend (through death or moving away)
  o Divorce (or breakup of a relationship)
  o Low self-image (not knowing one's true worth)

- We see movies and TV shows, watch videos, and hear songs on the radio of people boasting about and glorifying drugs and alcohol ("Gin & Juice", "I Get High…high…high…!", "I got my drink and my two step…" and "…pass the Courvoisier"). They make using drugs seem like the thing to do!

Once is all it takes for many! Drugs are addictive—and alcohol *is* a drug!

Open your eyes…Face the truth!

Drugs lure you in (make you feel good); then traps you! Once ensnared, it won't (easily) let you go!

Addicts will lie; cheat; steal; and sell their property, the property of others and their own bodies to get a hit.

No one says to him or herself, *"I want to be a crack head!"* or *"I have found my goal in life! I'm going to be a "meth-addict"… "a syrup head"… or "a heroine junky!"*

Addicts that do not obtain help:

- End up in jail
- Contract various diseases (through extended drug use, sharing needles, unprotected sexual activity due to poor judgment) and the inevitable malfunctioning of their bodies' organs
- Are killed by their habit or are murdered due to some drug-related incident

Change your mind! Get help!

Some drugs are natural but when eaten, smoked or snorted can cause sickness and even death!

Consider this:

During the summer, no one, after experiencing the heat of the day, quenches his or her thirst by drinking a tall cool glass of ammonia! Ammonia is natural, yet if one were to consume it, one would become very sick and quite possibly die.

One might say, *"But some drugs are natural, especially weed! It's from the earth!"*

Well, poisonous arrow frogs are natural; but if you were to eat one of them—you'd die! Poison ivy and poison oak are also natural! No one willingly messes with them! With the exception of a meteorite here and there, everything on (planet) Earth is "earth", however not everything is safe for man to eat, smoke or partake of!

One may counter with, *"Well, I have heard that doctors prescribe marijuana to their patients who suffer with glaucoma!"*

This statement is correct yet one must understand that this drug is being regulated (it is still dangerous). If one were to take more than the recommended dosage of aspirin, one would run the risk of hurting one's self, possibly dying. The same thinking applies with smoking marijuana. Because marijuana is prescribed to a person (in regulated doses) does not take away the drugs' potentially harmful effects. Marijuana cigarettes have up to four times the cancer-causing agents of cigarettes and causes short-term memory loss. Besides, a person is labeled as an addict because his or her drug consumption far exceeds the recommended or normal usage. This is why it is known as drug abuse!

One might say, *"Then doing drugs is okay just as long as I don't go overboard!"*

But there is the trap!

Drugs are addictive! They lure you in by their appeal and then (without warning), clamp shut like bear a trap!

Some snakes have the type of venom that doesn't kill; rather, it slowly paralyzes its victim within a minute or two. The animal that has been bitten attempts to run but can only go but so far before the venom renders it immobile. The snake, in turn, exerts little effort to catch his prey and slowly swallows it whole. It is the same with humans who become addicted to drugs!

Don't start! Why press your luck? It's like playing Russian roulette! Doing drugs can blow your brains out!

A little more to think about!

Have you ever noticed the connection between drugs and what is called witchcraft?

Open your eyes…Face the truth!

Watching various television shows and movies has opened my eyes to the truth concerning this matter. Because it has been made to look comical or ridiculously outlandish, most of us (the viewers) naturally dismiss witchcraft as fantasy, never giving it serious thought. However, witchcraft does exist and is very real!

What's the best way to advertise an immoral concept or clearly harmful product (something that is illegal, unhealthy or wicked)?

The answer: slip it into TV and radio programming—make it a hot topic in social media; write it into song lyrics; and mix it into movies, video games and everything that that our youth will come in contact with (not only the youth but also the ignorant, uniformed, and the foolish)! Bombard them; saturate their environment and their minds with products and programming that promote the desired (negative) results.

If a child is taught to think in a certain way or to do anything as a habit, he/she will continue in this manner well into his his/her adulthood.

Look at the similarities between what is seen on television and reality regarding witchcraft and drugs/alcohol.

- Love potions—created to make one fall in love with the first person one sees!
  - Ecstasy, Mollies, etc., gives one heightened sense of pleasure from being touched and is called the love drug!
  - Spanish fly is used primarily in date rapes! By slipping some of these drugs into a person's drink, one can be very easily talked into performing sexual acts!

- Strength and endurance—created so that one can do more, go longer, be stronger!

  - Steroids supposedly help build strength and endurance (but its users also experience what is known as "roid rage"—a side effect that could cause them to lash out in fits of anger, even commit murder!).

o Speed/uppers increase one's abilities, helps one to stay awake and accomplish more (but when your body crashes from exhaustion, you "Crash" hard!).
o Malt liquor creates boldness and arouses anger and a violent temperament. This is what is known as the rams (wanting to fight)!
o Viagra (yes, even this) increases male potency!

Need we go any further?

Almost all drugs have harmful side effects, especially when taken in excess or beyond what has been recommended. Again, drugs are very addictive!

Consider this!

We've all seen the spy flicks! James Bond or some other spy type is captured! Strapped to a chair and denied both food and sleep, the spy is forcefully persuaded to talk (divulge secret information). Finally, the now frustrated bad guy resorts to the use of truth serum (drugs). The result, with the exception of 007, is that the truth serums so weakens the spy's mind that he or she spills all of the beans. In similar instances, people are literally reprogrammed or brainwashed, having their minds and memories altered and their lives and lifestyles completely changed. How is this done? Is this so far-fetched? Isn't this the same thing that happens to us when we drink/use drugs and listen to certain songs over and over again? The mind is weakened due to lack of sleep and or drug consumption, bombarded repeatedly with visions, stories and ideas of sex, drugs and or violence until eventually, what is seen and heard is acted out.

Our behavior reflects the programming that we have been exposed to most!

Finally

What (do you think) is meant by this phrase "wine and spirits" (which hangs over the doors of the stores that sell liquor)? The "wine" part is understandable enough—but what on earth is the "spirits" portion talking about? HMMMMM...

Open your eyes…Face the truth!

Wine is a mocker, strong drink [is] raging: and whosoever is deceived thereby is not wise. (Proverbs 20:1)

Who has woe? Who has sorrow? Who has strife? Who has complaining? Who has wounds without cause? Who has redness of eyes? They that tarry long over wine; those who go to try mixed wine. Do not look at wine when it is red, when it sparkles in the cup and goes down smoothly. In the end it bites like a serpent and stings like an adder. Your eyes will see strange things, You will be like one who lies down in the midst of the sea, like one who lies on the top of a mast. "They struck me," you will say, but I was not hurt; they beat me, but I did not feel it. When shall I awake? I must have another drink." (Proverbs 23:29-35)

And be not drunk with wine, wherein is excess; but be filled with the Spirit; (Ephesians 5:18)

The acts of the flesh are obvious: sexual immorality, impurity and dishonesty; idolatry and witchcraft; hatred, discord, jealousy, fits of rage, selfish ambition, rebellions, divisions and envy; <u>drunkenness</u>, orgies, and the like. I warn you, as I did before, that those who live like this will not inherit the kingdom of God. (Galatians 5:19-21) NIV

Addiction

Open your eyes…Face the truth!

Understanding Addiction

In the preceding chapters, we have mentioned "addiction" when referring to drugs/alcohol and have hinted to other addictive behaviors. Each day, more and more individuals fall into *addiction*. Many of those individuals will spend a lifetime attempting to break free from addiction's viselike grip.

But what exactly is addiction? How can it be conquered?

Addiction is mental enslavement to a particular behavior or substance (drugs/alcohol), which compels an individual to surrender his or her body to (the behavior or substances') demands.

Addiction is a mental dependency (reliance, craving) for something (usually harmful), which cannot be satisfied. The more one does to appease one's addiction, the more one hungers for it.

How does one become addicted? Where does it start?

- One might become addicted (through first time) experimentation with drugs/alcohol, sex, or some other behavior.
- One may become addicted through extended exposure to certain substances or behaviors that one has found to be pleasurable.
- A habit (some frequently repeated action) may become a *stronghold* (semi-permanent way of thinking), which requires help and is nearly impossible to overcome.

A habit can be broken through one's actions—by disciplining one's self (through practice) to create a positive routine. A stronghold is psychological (mental). An addiction is a *stronghold* that has taken over the body as well. It is both psychological (mental) and physiological (how the body functions). If the mind is not changed or given a new direction, the stronghold will continue to push the addict toward destruction!

"Habits and strongholds are the same!" one might say. However, they are not. A habit can be likened to a pond or lake; a stronghold is like an ocean! A habit can be broken with practice; a stronghold requires a great deal of help (and for some, their addiction might never be broken).

Addiction is a *stronghold.*

At the very heart of every kind of addiction is the need for love and acceptance!

Addiction preys on our insecurities (fears), our need to belong and our need for a close and meaningful relationship!

One opens him/herself to addiction when one attempts to fill a particular void on the inside with a substitute from the outside!

Addiction hides within something that makes the individual feel good (temporarily). It lowers our defenses by presenting itself as something harmless or entertaining. The individual begins to use that substance or thing a coping mechanism; an outlet—a comforter to deal with the various stresses of life. The greater the stress or pain—the more the individual relies on that *'false comforter'* to make him or her feel 'good'. The snare of addiction then springs shut like a bear trap! By the time the individual realizes that he or she is trapped and that the addiction is killing them, they are unable to get free or stop!

(For example, one may be sad, depressed or lonely; therefore, to fill that void, one begins to eat more and more.)

- Addiction preys on those who are:

    o Grieving—over a loss, someone moved away, breakup of a relationship, or death (drugs offer false comfort)
    o Hopeless—feeling that their present condition can never and will never change
    o Lonely—having no companion and no one to talk to or share ideas with, feeling that no one understands, feeling isolated, etc.
    o Of low self-esteem—not having a positive image or understanding of one's own worth (feeling ugly, useless, undesirable, unintelligent, unlucky, etc.)
    o Fearful—having the inability to cope with stress (taking tests, making deadlines, dealing with or managing people, etc.)
    o Foolish or ignorant—the curious, those who don't think that they will become addicted, those lacking understanding of the danger, those having no knowledge of their family's history with addiction

Low self-esteem, peer pressure, grief, depression and ignorance are the doorways to addiction!

One who is insecure, does not know where he or she stands and does not understand his or her own worth, is a sure candidate to fall into some kind of addiction. One's search for acceptance, relief from pain, stress or depression may lead one straight into the powerful embrace of addiction!

Addiction is a trap hidden within something that looks, feels or tastes— good! (The saying *"Don't let the smooth taste fool ya!"* applies here!)

Addiction is like a fish hook, pulling the individual that has taken its bait to his or her death!

Addiction locks the addict on to a particular course that he or she is unable to turn away from or stop! (Imagine being tied up in a speeding car, and you are in the driver's seat. There is no steering wheel or breaks, and there is a brick wall or cliff ahead!)

There are many kinds of addictions.

- Social Media/internet (Various chat sites, blogging, texting/sexting, etc.,--must check who made a comment, who liked your comment or pictures, etc.)
- Anger (sarcasm, verbal abuse, jealousy, bitterness, rage, violence) leads to scars, wounds, suspensions or dismissal from job, loss of friends and family, isolation, jail time, death.
- Sex (pornography, masturbation, casual sex [with multiple partners]), which leads to abortions, multiple children (with different and--in many cases, absentee fathers), sexually transmitted diseases, homosexuality, rape, molestation, sickness and infections that may be incurable and even cause blindness and death.
- Gluttony (overeating) leads to obesity, clogged arteries, diabetes circulatory problems and death.
- Drugs/alcohol (consuming/using caffeine, cigarettes, marijuana, heroin, cocaine, crack, ecstasy (Molly), K-2, beer, wine, chewing tobacco, prescription drugs, etc.) leads to loss of job, lack of money, debt, theft, prostitution, loss of family and friends, and sickness (harms the brain, liver, lungs, heart, throat, gums, bladder, circulation, and may cause death)
- Gambling (placing bets on horses, boxing, all sporting events, dice, cards, casino games, etc.) creates debt, which results in unpaid bills, family conflicts, loss of job, the shutting off of utilities and evictions, theft, prison, potential physical harm (from those seeking payment).
- Shopping (clothes, shoes, hats, power and digital equipment) results in debt; buildup of unpaid bills, shutoffs and evictions, bad credit.
- Theft (kleptomania, robbery) leads to jail time, physical harm and debt.
- TV (soap operas, talk shows, game shows, cartoons, etc.) results in undeveloped or underdeveloped social skills, clouded perception of reality (views every situation, relationship, and problem through what was seen on TV) and over time, various physical problems from lack of exercise.
- Lying (gossip, slander, bragging, exaggerating, fraud, deception) leads to various and many afflictions, loss of friends, broken relationships, violence, jail time, death

- Games (videos games, etc.) results in unproductiveness, lack of vision, lack of goals, laziness, impatience, lack of focus in school or job, (potentially) unemployment or underemployment, (perhaps) turning to "get rich quick" schemes, like drug selling, resulting in jail time or death.
- People (family members, mom or dad, boyfriend, or girlfriend, spouse) may cause one to live to please others, to have low self-esteem, to feel one cannot manage without the person (being) around, to be possessive with friends and other relationships, resulting in jealousy, depression, overeating, drug/alcohol use suicide, bitterness, violence, even murder!

Once again, the root of addiction is the need to feel fulfilled through the love and acceptance of other people! One feels pressure or *'fear'* because one sees one's self as inferior, not looking, dressing, and acting like others, not being good enough, smart enough, tall enough, etc.

Many people return to their addiction in times of stress and pain.

One may have had a hard day or week for that matter, at work; one may have just failed an important test, have been in an argument or have experienced a breakup with one's boyfriend, girlfriend, or spouse. All of these are triggers that influence us to return to our addictions.

"This is crazy!" "This is foolish!" or *"How stupid!"* one might think. *"Why would anyone return to the thing that was once killing them? Why would they revisit the source of such great pain and confusion?"*

We return to our addictions because, for a few brief moments, we find an escape and relief however small. For a few brief moments, there is no pain; no grief; and no feeling of loneliness, awkwardness, or inadequacy. One might say, *"For just a few moments… I feel good!"*

When one is in pain or loses hope, all one wants is relief. It is amazing what we will do, the lengths we will go to, in order to alleviate or avoid pain. My mentor once told me that *"Our whole lives are spent in the pursuit of pleasure and in the avoidance of pain."* Therefore, we should not look down on the addict; his/her desires are normal. It is the method or path that the addict has chosen to fulfill his or her desires that is leading him or her down the path toward (self) destruction. They must be shown the truth about their situation, and then they must desire (wholeheartedly) to remove themselves from that deadly path and on to one, which leads to life and peace.

Addiction—the temporary, (false) 'comforter'—must be replaced by (real) 'love'. The false substance, person or thing must be completely rejected and the true 'Comforter' must be willing received.

The individual with the addiction must come to realize that he or she is loved, accepted—even forgiven, despite their shortcomings (that are outside of the addiction). Until the individual comes to trust and embrace true love, that person will continue in the downward spiral of addiction. Only by realizing and then choosing to turn to the true 'Comforter' in times of stress and pain, will the individual begin to conquer addiction.

Example: *A child, moved from foster home to foster home may become angry, rebellious and violent (as his/her coping mechanism). However, that same child is adopted by loving parents. At first, that child behaves negatively (coping mechanism). After some time, the child realizes that these parents really do love him or her—and that this home is permanent. The child relaxes and releases his or her pent up anger and hurts. The child's behavior changes! This doesn't happen overnight. However, it is the same with addiction!*

Once an individual finds true, unwavering love and is fully persuaded of that fact—addiction comes to an immediate stop. However, one must turn away and avoid the persons, places, and substances that are associated with their illness—and begin to walk in the opposite direction of the path that was leading him or her toward self-destruction.

Note: *Although one has turned around and is now walking in the opposite direction that they once were going, for some time, the individual is still on that same (deadly) path! He/she will stumble, fall at times—and become weary; unsure of one's self during the time he/she remains on that path. Yet something happens as one walks. One begins to find strength; one's confidence begins to build! During the process, one begins to understand where he/she has gone wrong, why they have ended up on this path of destruction. In time, the individual will find that the addiction no longer holds him/her and that he or she is no longer on the path, which leads to death and destruction. Now he/she* *is treading on the path which leads to life! One's life begins rebuilding almost without effort! This is a process. However long it takes, learn to appreciate the process! The understanding and the growth alone is worth it!*

When one becomes sure of one's self—who he/she is and where he/she stands—addiction's grasp will be loosed!

When one finds an unwavering source of love and acceptance that fills the void in one's heart, one's addictions will cease!

If we can redirect our focus; somehow being taught or gaining understanding that we are indeed loved and accepted(being comforted in the fact)—and if we can come to love and accept ourselves, addictions will be eliminated completely!

Love is the key! We must learn to love ourselves. We must learn to forgive others (those who have offended us) as well as forgive ourselves. We must resist fear (we've discussed this before) and conquer our guilt/shame, realizing that no one is perfect and that we all make mistakes. We must realize that gaining freedom requires understanding our current condition, rejecting it, changing how we think and working toward a greater goal. Furthermore, we must keep at it no matter how many times we fall. Lastly, we must understand that change takes time and will not happen overnight.

We all are seeking unconditional love! (Love and acceptance that won't change; get old or ever be taken away from us).

The void (that we feel inside of us) is our longing for a deep, loving relationship!

Who is able to fill that void and give peace to our souls?

There is one who is able!

For all that is in the world—the desires of the flesh and the desires of the eyes and pride in possession—is <u>not</u> from the Father but is from the world. (1 John 2:16 ESV)

All things are lawful for me, but not all things are helpful. All things are lawful for me, <u>but I will not be enslaved by anything</u>. (1 Corinthians 6:2 ESV)

Submit yourselves therefore to God. Resist the devil, and he will flee from you. James (4:17 ESV)

Beloved, I urge you as sojourners and exiles to abstain from the passions of the flesh, which wage war against your soul. (1 Peter 2:11 ESV)

"Therefore, come out from among them and be separate, says the Lord. Touch no unclean thing, and I will receive you." (2 Corinthians 6:17-Berean Literal Translation)

Jesus answered them, "Truly, truly, I say to you that everyone practicing the sin is a slave to the sin. (John 8:34- Berean Literal translation.)

So if the Son shall set you free you will be free indeed. (John 8:36- Berean Literal translation.)

Open your eyes...Face the truth!

A daydream

One day in the future we'll stop playing with guns.
Holding street corners hostage in pursuit of 'stacking ones'
No more shots will be let off, mothers jumping in coffins,
Families mourning their lost sons...
This happens too often!
One day, kids will play in the streets again!
And 'though conflicts arise, they won't kill their friends!
Question, does a gun 'truly' protect...?
Does it create a force field that makes bullets deflect?
Truth: We're killing our youth—and destroying our future!

Another child got struck down—"bucked down" by some clown...!
Come on y'all—let's put the guns down!

Let's stop killing each other.
Quit warring over corners.
Let's embrace our brothers—and uplift one another!
It takes one to 'spark it',
So I'll start it! (No doubt)
I keep it real, yo...!
But I'm *"chill"* though
(That's what I'm about!)

Written by: I. L. Jackson

I. L. Jackson

Anger

Open your eyes...Face the truth!

(D)Anger

We belong to an angry, frustrated, bitter and increasingly hopeless generation. Look around! You can hear the anger in the music; you can see it in the movie theaters and on television. You can see it on the Facebook, Instagram and other social media posts. You can see the frustration on the faces of both men and women struggling to provide for their families, being unemployed or underemployed. You can see frustration on the faces of our mothers who continue to raise their children with little or no support from the children's fathers and also on the faces of the youth who grow up in the same households as their angry, frustrated and embittered parents. Moreover, an increasing number of youth are directly affected by mental, physical and or sexual abuse; neglect, as well as drug/alcohol-addicted family members living in their households and in the surrounding communities. All such things nurture their feelings of anger.

We are living in a culture whose people are operating in "survival mode". Anger has become one of the two strongest and most frequently displayed emotions (the second is lust, which is not actually an emotion).

What is anger?

Anger is the strong emotional response to displeasure or dissatisfaction; it is the feeling of rage, indignation (vexed, hot, heated, etc.).

Anger is what we feel when someone has done something or something has happened that we do not like!

- Someone has taken or stolen from us (like money, our rights, freedom)
- Someone has violated us (hit, kicked or touched us in a way that we do not like)
- We have witnessed or have experienced an act of injustice (lied on, rights not upheld, betrayed (cheated on), bullied, falsely accused)
- Dissatisfied or disappointed (our expectations were not met; we were lied to)
- Someone has offended us (said something that hurt us or did something that caused us pain)
- Something bad happened to someone or something we care for

Anger is triggered by stress!

Stress is *"fear"* (it just keeps showing up) that manifests as:

- Pressure- from deadlines, living up to expectations
- Mental tension- uneasiness of the mind, continuous grappling with the possibility of falling short; that a goal will not be met; failing
- Anxiety (worry)- fretful over the possibility of something negative happening
- Frustration- feeling thwarted; that one's progress has been blocked; and all one's knowledge, wisdom and efforts have come to naught

What causes stress?

- Inner conflict
  - How I look, act *("I don't like my nose", "I'm fat", "I don't like the way I . . .", or "I'm just stupid!"*
  - What am I accomplishing? *("It's taking too long", "I'm not getting anywhere" or "Their holding me back!")*
  - My future *("Who will I be?" or "What will I do?")*
  - The desire to be accepted *("What do they think of me?" or "Does he or she like me?")*

- o Fear of failing or looking bad *("I can't do this!"* or *"They'll laugh at me.")*
- Changes
  - o Loss of a relative/friend
  - o Moving to a new home
  - o New job or loss of job
  - o New school

- Situations
  - o Worrying about money (*"How will I pay the bills?"*)
  - o Family/friend in trouble
  - o Learning/skill problems
  - o Peer pressure
  - o Deadlines (reports, assignments, etc.)
  - o Criticisms—being criticized, teased, mocked or made fun of

- Conflicts with others
  - o Friends/family
  - o Teachers
  - o Bosses/coworkers

A conflict is an argument or disagreement between opposing ideas, groups or sides.

Conflicts are a necessary part of life!

Through conflicts we are forced to grow and mature!

What causes conflicts?

There are four factors that cause conflicts:
(The original source is unknown)

- Unmet basic needs- lack of food, clothing, shelter, clean air, drinkable water, etc.
- Limited resources- scarcity of land, trees, drinkable water, money, oil, etc.

- Differing values- beliefs, morals, ideals of what is bad or good, traditions, etc.
- Bullying- intimidation, harassment, mistreatment or oppression of someone weaker, usually without a cause

(Every conflict can be traced back to the four factors listed above.)

Most conflicts are neither good nor bad. It is how we respond to them that determines the outcome.

Everyone deals with conflicts differently. We must be aware of this fact in dealing with and relating to individuals we may get into conflicts with.

There are six possible characteristics that can be exhibited when in a conflict. Everyone—man, woman, boy and girl—will display one of these six character types when confronted with a dispute. They are as follows: *force, revenge, sarcasm, withdrawing negotiation, and solving.* Below, I have put my own spin on these conflict characteristics. I learned about them during several prevention trainings and now (to make them more interesting and to have a little fun), I have connected these six traits to some familiar comic book characters! ***Comic book characters are taken from both Marvel and DC comics**

The Hulk/Phoenix (represents "force" or "rage"). This individual wants things his/her way and will smash anyone that stands in opposition! His/her way of solving conflicts is to force his/her will upon those he/she comes in conflict with through threats and violence. Once angry, there may be no reasoning with such a person. He/she will swell up change color, go berserk and destroy everything in sight! The only way to deal with such a person is to leave him or her alone; allowing them to calm down. (Those who consistently display this characteristic in dealing with conflicts often find themselves in trouble; imprisoned or dead.)

Batman/Mystique (represents "revenge"). This individual may give the impression that "all is well" and that the conflict has been resolved. However, in this person's mind, it will never be resolved until he or she feels that it is! In fact, such a person may dedicate his or her entire life in the pursuit of "getting even". When those whom he or she has had a conflict with are not expecting, this individual shows his or her true colors and strikes (as if from the shadows).

Open your eyes…Face the truth!

Warning: *There is an old saying that goes, "What goes around comes around," and this (vengeful) person may find that his/her vindictive nature has landed them in a world of trouble!*

Spiderman/Storm (represents "negotiation"). This person's motto is, *"I'll scratch your back, if you scratch mine!"* This person desires to solve the conflict by having both sides get what they want! He/she is willing to negotiate to come to a solution so that everyone wins!

Professor X/Wonder Woman (represents "solving"). This person desires to resolve conflicts by confronting the problem head-on but peacefully and truthfully (through brainstorming and working things out). He/she will not stop until the both sides have their desires met and the problem is completely eliminated! They will in no way compromise their morals or beliefs!

The Joker/Harley Quinn (represent "heckling" or "sarcasm"). These pranksters use teasing and busting to annoy and frustrate those they come into conflict with. Such persons don't *want* to get into a physical confrontation; however, he/she will beat their adversary with their wit and words! (Sometimes words hit harder than a fist. This person's words hit like a sledge hammer!) This individual's mouth often gets them into a lot of trouble!

Night Crawler/the Invisible Woman (represent "withdrawing"). When conflicts arise, this person tends to disappear. Not wanting to deal with the situation, they hope it vanishes as well! (However, he or she is usually the one person that attempts to shield friends or pull them away to safety when things get too hot or out of control!)

How do you respond to conflicts? (Think about it.)

Some expressions of anger are as follows:

- Outbursts and yelling
- Blaming
- Verbal abuse—cursing, put-downs, threats
- Sarcasm
- Silent treatment
- Temper tantrums—kicking, screaming, throwing, and breaking things

- Physical violence—rage, wrath, madness
- Revenge
- Murder!

Anger is a natural emotion.

To get or feel angry is natural. However, it is unnatural to always feel angry.

A person who is angry most of the time is living with hurts or disappointments that have not healed or been dealt with. These issues have been held on to (in many instances, for years), growing and festering, poisoning this individual's mind and body like cancer. Indeed, it is a cancer! Anger, in time, will become a root of bitterness if not dealt with and will continue to grow until it manifests as resentment and hate. This person may become violent even to the point of committing murder! Also, this anger will eventually consume and kill the individual (through destructive behaviors, ulcers, and other sicknesses).

A person may be frustrated. Frustration is a state of helplessness. One who is frustrated feels that he/she has tried and has exhausted all possibilities. This individual may have attempted to use reason, begging; going around, over, and under—yet all of his/her efforts have failed. There is only one option left and that is to become angry! Again, a root of bitterness will develop if this person continues to feel frustrated, which will eventually manifest as yelling, cursing and making threats. Violence and murder may soon follow! This is called madness!

"Mad" is the word used to describe animals that have gone crazy! (Such an animal, that has contracted rabies from the bite of another animal, has reached an uncontrollable state and has to be killed!)

Madness (uncontrolled anger) **should <u>NOT</u> be considered normal!**

However:

Anger is now being promoted as "gangsta", "thuggish", being a "goon" or a "monster", "ride or die"…etc.

Open your eyes…Face the truth!

- Social media- World Star, etc.
- TV/movies
- Songs and rap lyrics, etc.

The promotion of anger (rage) as an effective method of problem solving is causing an upsurge of violence, abuse, imprisonment and murder (even among females).

Anger has become the norm! Violence and murder continue to rise! This should not be!

Consider this!

Anger may start off quite small, like a seed. At some point, there was an initial incident that sparked the fires of anger! Perhaps someone said or has done something to hurt us. Perhaps they did not fulfill a promise. Over time, perhaps as more was said and done and more promises broken, the seed or fire grows! Here's the kicker—because most of us hold on to those hurts and disappointments—the seed of anger takes root and the fire continues to burn (simmering just under the surface). A seed needs nourishment and fire needs fuel in order to grow. Now, introduce social media, television, movies and music, laced with violent scenes and volatile, hostile lyrics that feed those flames! We watch and listen intently as their rage feeds our own! We say, *"That's what I'm talking about! He or she is where I'm at! They understand!"* The problem never gets solved; it is only discussed over and over again!

Side note:

Have you ever talked with a friend about some wrong that was done to you—and the more you discussed the matter, the angrier you became (and maybe they became angry as well)? Well, when we rehearse something over and over again, we become more familiar with it! We keep the offense alive! When we watch a movie/video or listen to music that reminds us of what we went through or what has happened to us, we intensify the hurt, we strengthen the anger and are overtaken by that feeling. In time we lash out (in some way or another)!

We must find a solution to the problem, not continue to rehearse it! Most people expend their energy pointing to or pointing out their problem(s). Addressing the problem is merely the first step—but very few people are willing to come up with a plan to resolve the matter and then put that plan into action. That's why they remain angry.

Over time, the seed (of anger) begins to flower and the *fruit* of it begins to show up in our actions. It may begin as sarcasm or some minor form of vandalism; perhaps it will come out in the form of profanity. Anger begins to manifest physically. Like anything that is well fed, the more we nourish anger the larger and stronger it becomes. The fire (called anger) blazes and the seed will eventually mature into a full grown tree, eventually bearing its fruit! The fruits of anger ripen and fall, more of the same seeds are planted in our hearts, going through the same process as the first until eventually there is an entire forest. (Fruit have seeds within them, therefore they reproduce infinitely!)

The fires of anger (if left unchecked) will rage hotter and hotter until it can no longer be controlled. The result is violence!

"(D)estructive behavior +Anger = (D)anger!" –**Reggie Byers**

Let's talk about violence.

Someone once said that *"violence is the manifestation of a deeper issue,"* and that is true!

Myth: Violence is a learned behavior.

Fact: Violence is an inherent trait in all of us!

Violence doesn't need a reason to happen. Violence doesn't need a cause!
Ask anyone who has been 'jumped' (beaten-down) while waiting for the bus or train.

Violence is *not* a learned behavior despite what "experts" have concluded. You neither have to teach anyone to be violent—nor does anyone have to witness violence in order to become violent.

Open your eyes...Face the truth!

Case in point: Place two or more small children in a room together. Add a toy (or something interesting to the children). Eventually, one of the children will attempt to keep the toy away from the other(s). The children that desire to hold the toy will soon begin to cry out of frustration. If these children are left to themselves (having no one to cry to), one child will resort to hitting; and if no one interferes, a fight may occur.

Were these children taught this behavior? Did they see it on social media, TV or hear it on the radio? Did they witness their parents in a knockdown, drag-out fight?

In most cases, the answer is **NO!**

The tendency toward or capacity to be violence is hardwired into us all (from the womb). However, the degree in which violence manifests differs from person to person. For some, the tendency toward violence is very strong. Since violence is directly attached to our emotions (anger), we might say of one person, *"He or she has a short fuse!"* or *"He or she is a hothead!"* In others, however, the tendency to be violent might seem almost nonexistent. Of such people, we say, *"So and so wouldn't* (or couldn't) *hurt a fly!"*

Myth: Violence or negative behavior begins in the home.

Fact: Violence and negative behavior does not always start in the home.

Some bullies, violent individuals and those that practice negative behaviors come from pleasant, peaceful homes (I know of such individuals). Although home is a major factor in an increasing number of cases, let us look at the matter realistically.

Some people:

- Are naturally grumpy—From the moment they emerged from the womb, they were ill-tempered and crabby
- Have or develop mental disorders—Bipolar Depression, Schizophrenic, Intermittent Explosive Disorder, etc. (due to seeing or experiencing trauma, which is not necessarily in the home)
- Impulsive—Emotionally high-strung (having an explosive temper)

- Some individuals are strong-willed, prideful—always desiring to have his or her way, unwilling to receive correction (incorrigible). Such a person will lash out!
- Just plain evil—some people are mean-spirited and wicked from the womb. Doing wrong and being violent is viewed as fun. There is no reason; it is just an expression of who they are.

Ideally (however) . . .

Violence is the negative reaction to stress, anger, frustration, jealousy, helplessness and or hopelessness!
What an individual has seen or experienced in the home may be a factor, which leads to violent behavior (outside of the home); however, a person may find that he or she can use violence to control others (through intimidation). This is called bullying.

A growing number of people use violence as the tool by which they achieve power and respect (adopting the same methods as organized crime).

Our culture has become a breeding ground for violence!

As I have stated previously, violence does not always originate at home. A child may be reared in the most loving and nurturing of environments yet he or she may have the sort of disposition that causes him or her to lash out when angry. Perhaps when this child enters school, he/she realizes that because he or she is larger than his or her peers, he/she can control the other students by beating them up or making threats!

(Through news reports) we are finding out (more and more) that there doesn't have to be a reason for someone to commit a violent act or to behave in a negative way. It is a sign of the times!

Have you ever been in class (or remember when you used to go to school), sitting behind another student; and out of nowhere, the thought came to you to just slap him in the back of his neck or maybe it was to pull her ponytail?

Open your eyes…Face the truth!

Some of us have acted out according to those wicked thoughts and no one did or said anything to us! What was that? Why did we do that? We weren't angry. We didn't learn that at home. Hmmm…

We know that the potential to act out violently is hardwired into each of us; however, many of us do not practice violence (physically). We may however, lash out verbally. Unfortunately, violent behavior is increasing rapidly. This is due (in part) to the following factors:

- **The media** (TV, radio, movies, social media, video games, etc.)- broadcast, package and promote violence as a means of entertainment. We are *as* we think!

Do you remember what was said about the seed of anger and how it is nourished?

Violence is often a physical or verbal manifestation of anger. If someone is consistently exposed to violent programming, violent songs, as well as games, eventually, he or she will adopt the attitude that violence is the answer to all of life's conflicts. Although that individual may never act out (physically) he/she will accept it (the attitude) and influence others by what he or she says. Such a person will expose his or her children to this same mind-set through:

- **Immaturity**—Prone to lashing out and or giving full vent to his or her anger lacking self-control. Like a baby, such a person is displaying that he or she has not matured to the level of using reason to solve problems; this person has not learned or developed positive coping skills that can come through close interactions with different people on various levels.
- **Drugs/alcohol abuse** (which is spreading like an epidemic throughout our nation) hinders an individual's judgment; rendering him/her incapable of making wise decisions. The reaction to most conflicts end in violence because those who are under the influence act out of emotion.
- **Ignorance/lack of education/arrogance.** There are some who were never told or warned about violence or drug abuse. Still others are

knowledgeable about the dangers of drugs/alcohol and continue to indulge in risky behaviors. Why is this? They are arrogant!

Some just don't believe that they could get addicted or be seriously injured or even killed. The problem is not that they don't know; the problem is that they don't possess understanding! Many lack insight and can only see the tip of the iceberg concerning their actions or reactions. Children and those who are immature fail to perceive the hidden dangers that lie in wait below the surface of conflicts and situations. Concerning violence, most folk have not thought about how drugs/alcohol, what they watch and listen to, their own emotions and natural disposition, and what they have experienced contribute to how they deal with life's situations and conflicts. Sadly, because we (as a whole) remain unaware of the factors listed above, we continue to go our way down the path of destruction.

This is _not_ a trend. Therefore, it will continue to get worse before it gets better. Look around…

We must practice self-control.

Self-control is the ability to feel one way (angry, sad, sorrowful, etc.) yet not allowing how we feel to affect our conduct. This is not hiding what one feels; instead, it is maintaining clear thinking (judgment), restraining one's self from acting out *despite* what one feels.

We have discussed stress and its causes. We have also discussed that stress is a trigger for anger. Now let us continue to examine stress by looking at how it is or is not dealt with.

*(The following notes on responding to stress are taken from Christian Education Ministries.)

There are only two responses to stress:

- Reacting (out of emotions)
    o Upsetting thoughts
    o Fear—panic, anxiety, worry
    o Depression—sadness, suicidal thoughts

o   Helplessness—feeling that "there is nothing I can do!" "I can't move!" "I can't stop!" or "I can't change!"
o   Hopelessness—this (situation or circumstance) is the way it is and it is never going to change
o   Anger—outbursts, vandalism, verbal or physical violence

Reacting to stress usually leads to more problems because our emotions fluctuate with every situation. Sometimes they run high or hot, which can lead us to violence and trouble; or they can run low, which can sink us into deep depression, despair, and suicide.

- Responding (using patience, logic, reasoning)
  o   Positive self-talk
  o   Problem solving
  o   Relaxation, exercise
  o   Communicating needs
    ▪ Writing it out, sending a letter or note
    ▪ Talking it out
    ▪ Asking for someone to assist (mediate or arbitrate/judge) with the problem

Responding to stress affords us opportunities to grow (mature) as well as strengthen relationships with others. It helps us to maintain good (mental) health and is useful in assisting others to cope with life's problems and situations.

There are serious physical problems that are linked to stress, unresolved bitterness and anger.

- Stomach ulcers—holes created by excessive acid that has eaten away the stomach's lining due to the body always being in a state of crisis or defense mode
- Neck spasms and back problems—due to the body constantly being in a tense state, unable to relax
- Migraine headaches—due to stress, mind always in a state of anxiety, analyzing, worrying, etc. hypertension (high blood pressure)—due to the body being consistently in a hyper or excited state because of stress)

- Cancer—the formation of malignant tumors, which spread throughout the body, eventually killing the individual (may be caused by the buildup of poisons and stress, which cannot be released because the body is constantly in an agitated or tense state)

(We all must learn to, as Jasmine Guy [the actress who played Whitley in the sitcom *A Different World*], said "…relax, relate—and release")!

Forgiveness is a key in releasing anger.

We must learn how to forgive (and forgive completely)!

We cannot say, *"I forgive you, but I won't forget!"* That is not true forgiveness!

What we actually mean when we say, "But I won't forget!" is that whenever we deem it necessary, we intend to drudge up the offense and throw it into the face of the one that offended us. We use the offense as leverage to get our way and to wield power over the one whom we say we are forgiving. In actuality, however, we have not forgiven them; we are making them pay (severely at times) for hurting us. In many cases, we are as bad as or worse than those who have offended us. Their offense may have been a one-time action or inaction; however, our subtle revenge may be to punish them for years! Looking at it in this manner, I ask you, "Who (then) is more wicked, the original offender or we who have not truly forgiven? Ouch!

True forgiveness is restoring those that have offended us to the place they had with us before the offense.

If we cannot (truly) forgive from our hearts, then we ought not to lie as though we have. Don't even say, "I forgive you" if you don't mean it.

Forgiving others is very hard to do at times. It takes a lot of self-examination (sometimes switching roles, seeing things from another point of view) and practice. It is very hard to restore someone who has hurt us deeply to the place that we held them before we were offended yet releasing them releases us! Holding on to hurts and anger affects our mental and physical health because our bodies fly into an agitated state whenever we come in contact with the person we have a grudge with. Some work with or even live in the same house with those they have not forgiven; therefore, their bodies are constantly in a tense, agitated state. When one's body continues to work under stress and cannot find rest, it will begin to malfunction and eventually shut down! For our own good, we must learn to forgive.

We've all offended someone at one time or another. We all have said or done something that has hurt someone that we care for. Maybe that person never forgave you—though you've asked for forgiveness. Maybe it is you that needed the other person to apologize—but they refused. Some would say, "Well, forget them then! I don't need them!" but that would be a lie! If we were honest with ourselves, we would admit that it *is* still a sore spot.

Maybe you were forgiven and you know you really screwed up. You might say to yourself from time to time, "I wouldn't have forgiven me yet he/she forgave me! They're crazy!" No. That's love! The feeling you received when you were forgiven and that comes to you when you remember that you are forgiven is the same feeling someone else would feel if you were to forgive him or her! (Hint, hint...)

Forgiving others eases the mind and relaxes the body! Thinking becomes clearer and the body is able to find rest!

What has made you angry?

Are you holding a grudge? If so, for how long have you been holding on to it?

Do you have some things you need to let go of? Are there some people you need to forgive?

Angry people make other people—angry!

An angry person is on fire! Leave an angry person alone or his anger may set you ablaze!

Warning: Anger is the father (source) of violence and murder!

However:

A soft (tender hearted, loving) answer will curve the rage of an angry person!

(Understand this!)

Energy is neither created nor can it be destroyed! (I remember learning this in science class.)

Therefore, the energy generated by being angry, if not direct or channeled into something positive, will emerge negatively; or it, having nowhere to go, will be internalized and over time manifest in some bodily malfunction or illness.

Energy *can* be transferred or redirected!

Negative energy can be redirected into something positive!

We have a choice! We do not have to act out negatively!

When angry, that energy can be used to do the following:

- Do arts and crafts
    - Write out your thoughts (poetry/rhymes, journaling)
    - Painting, sculpting, drawing
    - Build something (birdhouse, doll house, book shelf, etc.)

- Exercise—running, jumping rope, sit-ups, lifting weights, etc.
- Protest—stage a boycott, a sit-in or strike, organize and have a march (and other peaceful demonstrations)
- Playing a sport—basketball, tennis, boxing (hitting the punching bag or heavy bag)
- Cry—Going off somewhere on your own and just yelling or crying (letting your emotions out) is good and often necessary. (It isn't some punk move to cry!) Going off to be alone for a few minutes will allow you to de-escalate, think, and get it together.

-

(The idea is to burn off the built-up/pent-up energy without doing physical harm to ourselves or to others, including furniture, dishes, appliances, family members, pets, etc.)

Open your eyes…Face the truth!

Don't let anger destroy you! Don't let anger:

- Get you suspended or expelled from school!
- Get you fired from work!
- Send you to jail
- Get you killed!

What do you do when you are angry?

What has anger cost you?

Tips for Dealing with Anger
(Source unknown)

If you are angry:

Keep your cool! Ask (the person), "Can we talk?" (A good idea is to pull them aside so that you may talk privately. If you feel there is a chance of things getting out of control, bring someone with you that you know is fair to act as a mediator. A mediator is a person who is on neither side yet will help solve the conflict peacefully.)

Politely explain why you are angry. A person is more willing to listen to you when you are calm. Showing rage may cause the other person to become enraged! They will not readily listen to anything you have to say, and the situation could get ugly!

Ask

If the person understands why you are angry
For a change to be made or for compensation
The person how he or she feels about the situation

When someone is angry with you:

1. Keep your cool! LISTEN to what the other person is saying.
2. Let the person know if you do not understand (ASK the person to explain again).

3. Tell the person you UNDERSTAND.
    - APOLOGIZE
    - ASK if you can TELL YOUR SIDE

Conquer it!

1. Keep your cool! TELL the person what you want.
2. LISTEN to the response. (The person may disagree)
3. If you cannot agree, propose a COMPROMISE.
4. CONTINUE this process until you can reach an agreement.

Be ye angry, and sin not: let not the sun go down upon wrath: (Ephesians 4:26)

Wherefore, my beloved brethren, let every man be swift to hear, slow to speak, slow to wrath: (James 1:19-20)

Be not hasty in thy spirit to be angry: for anger resteth in the bosom of fools. (Ecclesiastes 7:9)

A soft answer turneth away wrath: but grievous words stir up anger. (Proverbs 15:1)

The sacrifice of wicked is an abomination to the Lord: but the prayer of the upright is his delight. (Proverbs 15:8)

Make no friendship with an angry man; and with a furious man thou shalt not go; (Proverbs 22:24)

Cease from anger, and forsake wrath: fret not thyself in any wise to do evil. (Psalm 37:8)

But I say unto you, That whosoever is angry with his brother without cause shall be in danger of the judgment: Matthew 5:22(a)

He that is slow to wrath is of great understanding; but he that is hasty of spirit exalteth foolishness (Proverbs 14:29)

The need and purpose of 'fathers'

The need and purpose of 'fathers'

Today's generation suffers from a great and terrible epidemic; its effect is the ever-increasing rate of single parent homes and the rotting away of the family structure as a whole. First, an increasing number of people no longer believe in the institution of marriage; instead, they opt to coexist or—to put it bluntly, shack up, unwilling to fully commit to one person or relationship. (The mentality here is that if things get too rough or one of the individuals becomes unhappy, for whatever reason, they can move on with little to no strings attached). Second, the very institution of marriage has been legally changed by the courts. They are attempting to redefine what it means to be married. This goes against how marriage has always been defined and practiced since the beginning of time (that being a man joined together with a woman for the purpose of having children). Those individuals that practice homosexuality (men having sexual relations with other men) and lesbianism (women having sexual relations with women) seek to change the definition of marriage so that it might justify their perverted lusts (not condemning anyone, just calling it what it is). Lastly, there is the ever-increasing divorce rate which is devastating to everyone in the family.

In most cases, when there are breakdowns in the family structure (for whatever reason), it is the man (the father/husband) that finds himself removed from the family.

Look at our inner cities. Our men (both young and old) face a number of factors that hinder (but not necessarily stops) them from what many people see as being successful or productive. (Success—is perceived as: you must have lots of money, a nice car and a big home).

Success is not necessarily possessing things but having positive [close and growing] relationships with friends and family, a life free from addictions, a good reputation and being a good manager over the things you have been given.

Some factors that hinder us from being successful may include the following:
- abuse or neglect at home;
- having no positive male influences to lead them in the right direction (which is why many end up joining gangs);
- lack of education; lack of exposure to the arts and culture (and opportunities in general that may spark a young man's interest in a career other than sports);
- unemployment, and underemployment (little or no opportunities for advancement);
- lack of support by women—(that disrespect and tear down *good men* because they):
  - do not drive big, expensive cars or lacks a car
  - do not have high profile jobs,
  - can't afford to provide them with the "finer" things in life (minks, diamonds, red bottom shoes, etc…)
  - make less money than their women

It is not this author's intention to point the finger at anyone; however, this author's desire is to give some defense to those males who are trying despite great odds to be men—and who are positive and influential in their communities. Also, this author must point out that the things stated above do not refer only to "men". Women have complained for years that some men, when they are blessed with money and power, leave the women that have helped them to get there—for someone younger, prettier, and (many times) of another race.

Let's return to my original thought.

Society itself—through what the media conveys, consistently belittles, downplays, disrespects and even snatches the role of the husband/father from him. In many of our favorite TV shows, men are portrayed as incompetent, misinformed, (sometimes) cowardly, weak-willed buffoons. Remember Al Bundy in '*Married with Children*', Homer Simpson in '*The Simpsons*', '*The Family Guy*', '*King of Queens*', '*Everybody Loves Raymond*', '*King of the Hill*', '*American Dad*'? (The list goes on). I understand that the characters in these shows are exaggerations or caricatures of reality; however, the wives on such shows are often portrayed as domineering (or controlling), sensible, and competent. Think again of how the husbands/fathers are portrayed in each show in comparison to the wives/mothers. With such pictures of men constantly saturating each viewer's mind, it is not hard to see how many (people) of our current generation have become convinced that the 'man' is good for nothing more than a sperm donor—and comic relief. He is not needed in the development of our children. (Thankfully) there are a few TV shows and movies that portray men in a positive light.

(Notice also that many of these programs are in the form of cartoons! Although such shows may have been made for adult viewers, our youth make up much of the viewing audience! (This is not by happenstance).

How much of an influence has Bart Simpson, for instance, had over the years concerning the increased disrespect displayed by children toward their fathers (talking back, defying orders, calling his dad by his first name, etc.)? I'm not trying to hate but....

Think about it!

Such programs have great influence upon society. At one time, much of what we learned and knew about the world was gained by what we watched on television. Now we have smart phones and tablets, information is gained and shared immediately through the internet and over social media. Both positive and (sadly) negative messages are relayed in the blink of an eye!

Also, (most) African Americans continue to play out the conditioning that was forced upon them through slavery.

Open your eyes…Face the truth!

Willie Lynch (whose last name is the source of the phrase "lynch mob") was a slave owner who devised a "fool proof method for controlling slaves." In his writings (on the bank of the James River in 1712), this evil man laid out his plan of how to keep African Americans functioning in a slave mentality even if and long after slavery is abolished "for at least three hundred . . . perhaps thousands of years." If we are honest with ourselves his "method" is still working its evil!

- Using fear, distrust and envy for control purposes. We fight amongst ourselves. *"Distrust is stronger than trust, and envy is stronger than adulation, respect or admiration."*

- Turn the old blacks against the younger and the young against the old. This has created a generation gap in which neither side is willing to listen. Valuable information, as well as knowledge and wisdom, is withheld or lost forever; therefore, learning is hindered and mistakes are repeated, help and assistance is refused, unity is destroyed and the family structure begins to break down.

- Use the dark-skinned slaves against the light-skinned slaves.

Plantation owners were encouraged by Lynch to rape the African women that they had enslaved. After doing this, the slave master would separate the lighter from the darker and show favoritism to the lighter. Because the lighter-skinned slaves were treated better, had better jobs and living arrangements, many became puffed up, thinking that they were better than the darker ones. The darker slaves in turn became envious and were offended (seeing that the lighter slaves were treated better and because of their poor treatment) by how the conceited lighter blacks acted toward them. Even to this day, black people desire to look more like whites, wanting straighter hair, lighter skin, even trying to lose their thick lips, big behinds, etc. (Ironically, the whites are attempting to look more like blacks!)

Even in movies, the darker-skinned blacks are usually viewed as the villain— or evil while the lighter-skinned blacks are depicted as the heroes.

- Use the female vs. the male and the male vs. the female. The process was to make the black female look down on the black man (as a provider and protector), looking to the slave master (employer, government system) and to herself for these things.

Large, strong and powerful black men (the leaders, the warriors and the defiant) were tortured, even torn apart in front of their wives and children. Even to this day, any black man who rises up and becomes too powerful will be killed or silenced! (Remember Dr. Martin Luther King and Malcolm X— Now consider [billionaire, entertainer] Michael Jackson and perhaps Bill Cosby). The wives, not wanting the same fate to befall their sons, raised their young men in fear and weakness of heart. Also, black women were forced to become the heads of their households, assuming the roles of provider and protector. Thus, we have the strong black woman and the passive (weak-willed) man!

The black woman is preferred over the black man, giving the African American woman more favor and opportunities than the black man. Keeping him oppressed, without opportunities and resources keeps the black woman dependent on the slave master (or employer) while simultaneously and subtly creating an attitude of superiority or conceit within her and contempt toward her mate—the black man.

Example: Black women graduate from high school and may be able to get a "white collar" job (in a business or law firm, etc.). Their jobs might give certain perks; assistance in returning to school and chances for advancement. In contrast, black men graduate high school and tend to find "blue collar" jobs (in warehouses, doing physical lifting or custodial work). There aren't always as many chances for advancement in such jobs. (This same attitude also dominates our churches—women showing more respect and submission to the pastor than to their own husbands. The pastor is often looked upon with great honor and receives the love, respect and service that the husband has never received but desperately needs and desires.)

In response, the (black) man, sensing his wife's disappointment (through her attitude and actions) and envying her ability to rise above him, may begin to resent her in his heart. His self-esteem begins to suffer. He may begin to act out negatively, like using drugs and alcohol, engaging in illegal activities, or committing adultery. In numerous cases, the (black) man reacts out of his own fear and insecurities. His wife, though she may make more money than he, may not feel negatively toward him at all. However, because of conditioning, the man may still feel inadequate and eventually lash out.

(Remember our discussion on *fear*? Notice how greatly we are affected by it? We must face and conquer our fears if we are to effect change!)

Return to the Willie Lynch effect

- You must always have your overseers (employers, managers, supervisors) distrust all blacks, but it is necessary that your slaves trust and depend on us.

To this day, this tactic remains alive and well. Look at how blacks are portrayed in the media (in music, in videos, in social media and on TV). Have you noticed? Our faults and negative traits are broadcast far more frequently than our accomplishments and our positive traits. The world views us as brutish, money hungry, drug addicted; uneducated thugs. What Willie Lynch did not foresee, however, is that the Americanized Africans would begin to create cultures in the midst of their oppressed state that would have the entire world following our lead! (Unfortunately, though, we have failed as a people to successfully capitalize and use our influence to our advantage.) Many of us continue to look to and depend upon our overseers to provide us with the things we need.

All of these factors shape society's outlook of the African American man and his role in our communities and in our households. Although this author is speaking from the urbanized African-American perspective, the respect and treatment of fathers is diminishing in other races and cultures as well.

Fathers are AWOL (absent without leave)! Although we ultimately blame the man, I beg you to consider the following:

Have you ever seen the movie *"Mrs. Doubtfire"*? Believe it or not, there are some men who have remained faithful to their spouses and not cheated or have not been abusive in any way. Yet because they have not lived up to the expectations of their wives (the knight in shining armor that they have read about in the romance novels and have seen on the daily soap operas); because their incomes have proven to be insufficient in giving their families a better lifestyle, they are rejected and—in some cases, divorced. Unlike *Mrs. Doubtfire*, many of these men lack the resources to disguise themselves in order to reenter the family and win back those whom they love.

Commercial: This author just realized something deeply disturbing—but it lends its self to what this author has been attempting to say. In that movie, the "father" (man) had to <u>ACT LIKE A WOMAN</u> in order to ultimately win the respect and love of his wife and regain his family. Woe...

Good men (that find themselves alienated from their families) are forced to find a new place to rest their heads. Confused, angry and just plain hurt, these men are now faced with surviving. A man, that may have already been struggling financially, is now forced to live with even less. This is because *'good men'* still attempt to give support to their children (although many are forced to do so through the courts, even if they have been giving support [on their own] all along).

The children suffer. Once again, I ask you to understand the following factors:

There is a difference between a "man" and a 'male'. We will deal with that later. However, a (good) man that is separated from his family:

- Has to find a place to live. He might have to move back into his parent's home, an apartment or—end up renting a small room—in a place that is not suitable for young children to visit. (He might be ashamed to bring them there.)
- He may work two jobs in order to pay for his new residence—and for expenses (support) where his children reside; therefore having little time for anything more. (Time spent with his children may be short and he may be too tired to stay awake during their visits—sad but true.)
- Might feel hurt, anger, shame and frustrated because those things he tries to do for—or in order to see his children often do not work.
- Might end up in jail, trying to hustle up enough money to feed himself and his children. (I am not promoting that a man should commit illegal acts; however, because of unemployment and underemployment, this is a factor that cannot be overlooked.)

Maybe the new girlfriend or wife wants nothing to do with another woman's children. Also, add to those things listed above—a difficult ex-wife or ex-girlfriend:

- That may poison the children's minds against the father (the man may also do his own poisoning. It goes both ways.)
- That becomes jealous if the man finds a new girlfriend or wife, and therefore makes it difficult for him to see or spend time with his children because she doesn't want any other woman around (her children).
- That asks for more money than the man can afford to give
  - forcing him to find some other means of making money
  - may cause him to become bitter and sadly, he begins to want nothing to do with her at all (thus the children are left alone as well)
- That seeks to hurt (punish) the man for whatever reason; attempting to destroy his reputation, job and whatever else.
- That may not allow the father to see his children if she doesn't get her way.

Truthfully, if he is not wrongfully incarcerated or dead, there is no excuse that can be made to justify a father's absence. I am not attempting to make excuses for the things that have been listed above. I am merely listing the various factors that contribute to this terrible situation in the downward spiral of the family unit. The truth often hurts and this fact, this author (being estranged from my daughter) is painfully aware of. Therefore, (practicing what I preach) I too will reach out and attempt to patch up my broken relationship (if it is not already too late).

Fathers tend to catch a bad rap (and many times it is deserved). However, prayerfully, we all will have gained some understanding and encouragement—and make the necessary corrections after reading this chapter!

Fathers are MIA (missing in action) and because the position of the dad in many homes remains vacant, we are now faced with the following unnerving truth...

…Someone else has (or will assume) the role of father in the lives of our children!

Mother, big brother or sister, uncle, gang leader, drug dealer, pimp, rock star, rapper or actor—even the child's best friend (down the street) may be taking the place of "Daddy" in the lives of our young ones!

What is a father?

- The source—the beginning of the family
- Provider—works to make sure that the family has the basic necessities for living (food, clothing and shelter). May often require the help of his spouse due to underemployment and/or high cost of living.
- Foundation—the strong base upon which everyone else in the family is built up and rests. (If the base is weak or is somehow taken away, whatever is built upon it shall eventually fall apart.)
- Protector—guardian, defender, cover, shield (against danger, intruder, etc.)
- Leader—the person at the front, guide, the one who has the vision for the family and determines, which way it shall go
- Priest of the family—studies, prays (seeks God's face for answers and for direction), teaches the family what he has learned from God. (Each individual member eventually becomes responsible for their own spirituality. Ultimately, people are going to do what they want to do. However, the father is responsible to train them as best as he can while they are under his authority.)

The father is the start of the family!
(Using the perfect scenario as an example)

- He initiates. He asks or says to the woman, *"Excuse me Miss…What's your name? …Can I take you out….?"* (*Like the Luther Vandross song*)!
- He (usually) pursues the woman to lay with her (sexually). He speaks sweet, flattering words, "runs game" (lies, making promises he may or may not intend to keep), spends money, writes poetry, sings, buys her things and so on.

Even though a child or a family may not be his plan, the man is the initiator!

He:

- Ejaculates—releasing his seed (sperm) into the woman which fertilizes the egg that she produces. (If sperm never leaves a man's body, then a woman's egg will not be fertilized, and thus, no baby will be produced; therefore, there will be no family.)
- Initiates whether or not there will *be* a marriage. If he *doesn't* ask…if he doesn't want to make that commitment, there will be no marriage. (Sadly, many women are still anxiously waiting for their significant others to marry them. This is a hard truth.)

A real father works (that means brings in money)!

- The father is responsible for the food, clothing and shelter of his family. (Chiefly—but not solely, he may need his wife's help. This is the reality in many households; especially African American households). *And—if he is a stay at home dad, <u>he works</u> in the home!*

- The family is built upon his shoulders. He is the head or leader but his position in the family is the foundation (the bottom, not the top). What the family is or will become depends on his leadership and guidance. The family is built upon him! (The father has an awesome responsibility!)

Without the father, the family becomes dysfunctional!

- The mother may become overwhelmed, forced to (try to) take on *both* parental roles.
- The family may run through a number of would-be (substitute) fathers or "rent-a-pops." (Mom may have several boyfriends that may not have the family's best interest at heart. Sadly, such men may be kept around because they may be of use financially (or to combat loneliness). The danger here is that such males might be abusive predators, desiring to spoil the family.)

I. L. Jackson

- The children lose valuable guidance, wisdom and protection (if the biological father possessed any positive attributes to begin with. It may be that the child is the result of a one-night stand, drunken encounter, an act of casual sex, adultery/cheating or other such act.) This is a hurtful truth for many children.
- A child may be forced to grow up too soon, becoming the man of the house, assuming a position he (or she) should not be made to handle.
- A child's self-esteem may suffer because
    o He/she may begin to feel that he/she is unwanted or unloved.
    o The child may feel that he or she is the reason for the break up and the father's departure from the home.
    o The child may become emotionally torn, perhaps silently grappling with feelings of anger, disappointment and loss. Such emotions might never be voiced—let alone addressed and dealt with. (Many children carry this pain and anger into their adult lives, relationships and into marriage.)
    o The child may become the sounding board for ill feelings directed toward Dad, which creates further emotional damage. The child may become the victim of such feelings because he or she favors Dad in appearance and/or behavior.
    o The child may feel slighted because the father has gone off and is now raising another family, not spending any time with him or her (anger, bitterness and resentment can arise).
    o The child may feel that he or she is less than his or her peers because *their* families remain intact; having both parents.
    o Step-Brothers and sisters, who are from the step dad, may receive more love, attention and affection.

Children need both parents (actively pouring into their lives) so that they may become well-rounded members of society! (I must state that there are many instances in which both parents are present and active yet their children—when they are old enough to make their own decisions choose to go astray.)

A woman needs to be involved in the raising of a girl who will become a woman; and a man needs to be involved in the raising of a boy in order for the boy to become a man.

A man does not understand the ways (thoughts/motivations) of a woman nor can a woman fully understand the ways of a man. Men and women think, react and relate differently (it is how we are wired from the beginning of creation). A woman, raising sons on her own may rear them up to be timid, soft, effeminate—or too hard! Also, women have a tendency to spoil their sons. Some women fear their sons because they and/or the son have realized that he is larger and stronger than she. Other women will go up side their son's head if he gets out of line. However, we can see where a man may be needed.

Some men might disagree by saying, *"My mom raised me by herself and I turned out well! I know that I am a man!"* However, such men tend to forget the influence that a coach (from playing sports), military experience, a male teacher or mentor has had upon them. Therefore, there may have been a male influence or *father figure* in their lives that helped shape them into who they are today!

When our fathers are out of position, the family becomes weak and vulnerable to attacks by predators (thieves, burglars, con artists, child molesters and other males whose intentions are to seduce, use and abuse Mom and perhaps the entire family!)

(Let's look to the animal kingdom to strengthen the thought presented in the previous statement.)

Example:

While on the hunt, lionesses are plagued by the persistent, irritating presence of hyenas. Although the lionesses hunt in packs, hyenas will follow them. Once the lionesses make a kill, the hyenas will harass them. The strategy of the hyenas is to give the lionesses no peace by their relentless picking. Their hope is to steal the lions' kill. Also, if the hyenas are able to isolate one of the lionesses from the rest of the pack, they *will* kill her! Given the opportunity, even the male lions will kill a lioness and spoil an unprotected family. Such is the case when the (human) father is not present in the home.

Attributes of a Father

There are many things that can be learned from watching the animal kingdom! For example, one can learn much by considering the ant. Without captain, supervisor or ruler, this tiny creature stores up provisions in summer, gathering its food at harvest so that there will be sufficient food for all to last through the harshness of the winter! We can also learn by considering the attributes of certain other animals. There are three such animals by which a man should pattern himself. By imitating and practicing the positive attributes of these animals, a man can make himself more confident, more responsible and more powerful (holistically)!

A father has the attributes of the lion, the eagle and the ox!

The lion represents protection, authority, power (in voice and presence), strength, and courage.

- Protection. One full-grown lion can drive away a pack of hyenas (the lions' archenemy) and will kill any that gets too close or proves too slow to escape his jaws! Male lions have large manes (hair around his head, neck, and shoulders), which make him hard to kill! When the lion is fighting or defending himself, his thick mane protects his neck (where the killing blow is usually delivered). A man/father must be able to fight on, to take many (mental) blows and to continue on. He is able to endure more than other animals because his head is protected!
- Power and strength. The lion is incredibly strong and is capable of killing animals that are larger than him. One swat from the lion's powerful claws can kill its victim. A father must be a strong defender of his family, able to protect them physically if necessary and also he must be able to tackle problems much larger than himself!
- Lastly, the lion's voice can be heard up to a mile away (so too a father's voice must be)! When a father or a true man speaks, it should be with confidence and directness. It should be something worth saying and should have far-reaching influence. A father or a real man speaks with authority and for what is right. He speaks bold and strong!

Side note (to any young man who may be reading this book):

A lion does not (always) have to roar or fight to prove he is a lion!

A man understands that there are times when he must raise his voice or use force but that it is not necessary to do so at all times (to prove his manhood).

A man may play, spar or box; however, he does not risk his life over small or petty differences.

The eagle represents authority, visions, strength, and flight.

- Vision. Foresight and insight (and hindsight), the ability to see beyond present conditions and situations, spots dangers from afar off, he is also able to look back and see clearly (learning from the past)
- Flight. The ability to rise above problems and circumstances. The eagle is truly a majestic bird and wondrous to see in flight. An eagle may soar for hours without flapping its wings—at all! Also, when bad weather approaches: eagles are known for catching the air under their wings so as to propel themselves upward, thus flying over the storm where the sky is calm and blue, just like an airplane!
- Strength. When a female eagle chooses her mate, she tests him by carrying a log that is about her size and weight high into the air. The female then drops the log. The male must catch the log before it hits the ground! If the male fails to catch the log, he is rejected. A man/a father must possess this attribute—able to catch and carry a weak or fallen family member, restoring them to their former place!

The ox represents strength, hard work, determination and protection.

- Determination. The ox has the ability to move forward despite great opposition. He is able to carry or pull a heavy load; likewise, a father should be able to pull or carry his family to where they need to go even after their strength has failed.
- Endurance. The ox is able to pull those that he is hooked up with for quite a distance and for long periods. This is meant by having endurance. A man/a father must possess this attribute!
- Strength. The ox works daily (often long and hard)!
- Protection. The ox is a fierce defender of his territory! If one were to step into an ox's pen, the ox will not hesitate to attack! (The notion about oxen/bulls seeing red is a myth). What provokes them to attack is

not the color red; it is the movement of anything that was not invited in. The ox's attack is relentless! His pursuit will continue until the intruder leaves or has been dealt with!

The attributes of these three animals are indeed essential for any man or father, yet there is one more attribute that is greater than these! This attribute is the very foundation upon which the others rest; it is that of a priest!

The priest represents a spiritual foundation, looking to "the Father of all" for guidance, strength and understanding. (A father must learn from the only good and perfect example of fatherhood—God!)

Life without the Father

Life for Boys

Without a father in his life, a boy may feel:

- Rejected, abandoned or unwanted—feels that Dad doesn't care for him or what he does because the father has little or no contact with him
- Anger and bitterness—stemming from disappointments, lack of attention, witnessing or experiencing abuse, seeing Dad repeatedly at his worse (angry, violent, drunk, high/on drugs)
- Depression—mourning the loss of his father as if his father had died
- Inadequate (lacking confidence) ill-equipped because Dad has not taught or set any example for him to follow (other than negative things).

Such factors give life to the following statements:

"I don't need him! He spends no time with me! He's drunk again! He's a coward! He hurt my mom; then he left! @*#$" him! I'll be my own man! I'll learn how to be a man on my own!"

A boy left to raise himself is very dangerous! He might turn to the streets, join a gang; become a drug dealer or pimp. He may learn how to scam and hustle, lie, cheat and steal (perhaps even commit murder). Such a young man might learn only to respect money and power—and will do what he must to get them. Although his goal may be to be nothing like his father, he will most likely become his father's spitting image or worse. His father may have learned all that he knows in much the same way. This is a vicious cycle or generational curse that needs to be broken!

Such a boy is likely to mistreat women and have babies by different mothers—unless his mother or some other adult holds a strong influence over him). What this author finds truly amazing is that there are growing numbers of (inner city) boys who are raised by their mothers yet—instead of having a deep respect for *all* women for the sacrifices and pain their mothers have endured in raising them, they do the complete opposite—degrading, using and abusing the very ones that will (someday) birth and raise their children.

The relationship between father and son is crucial to the son's development!

- The father is a counsellor and confidant (that is seeking his son's highest good). He is the one person that the son can go to and talk about his thoughts and feelings. A father will attempt to point his son in the right direction.
- The father helps to shape and establish the son's view of the world.
- The father encourages exploration and independence. The father will say, "Get up! And you can do it!" Mothers are built to nurture their children; fathers bring out a kind of positive tenacity from (within) his children.
- Even horseplay reinforces the bond between fathers and sons! The father challenges his son to run or play harder, go higher and do better by rolling up his sleeves and getting down and dirty (doing things with his children), showing them by example how something is done!
- The father shows the son how to interact and treat his mother (as well as all women).
- The father (in times past) would train the son up in the family business or at least teach him a skill that will help him make money.

Without his father, a boy grows up a frustrated and insecure 'male'.

A frustrated male is often a violent male!

The Life of a Girl Growing Up without Her Father

This is not as easily summed up because a girl's relationship with her father is something truly special. It is through her relationship with her father that she learns what to look for in a husband. Through her father, a girl experiences the tender side (the gentleness) of a man!

A woman that has been raised without a father tends to think that a man should be macho or thuggish (always hard), forceful, even angry and frustrated. This is the image she has seen on TV, in movies and in music videos. She carries this image into her relationships, marriage and in the raising of her children. If her husband or boyfriend fails to meet with this incorrect image of manhood, she will begin to reject him, claiming:

- *"He's too nice" or*
- *"I need a real man. He's weak!"*

Still, there are other women who had abusive, drug addicts or angry men as fathers. Such women, raising their children alone, may raise them to be effeminate timid and passive. Their children tend to be overly emotional, hot-headed and unbalanced.

Our girls are growing up with a warped image of men.

Through videos, music, social media, etc. –and the streets, many inner city girls learn that (all) men are angry, corrupt, abusive, ruthless and unfaithful cheaters. Therefore they are drawn to those males that are rebellious thugs and gangsters that handle all conflicts through anger and violence.

Many of our girls are looking for the love, attention and affection they did <u>NOT</u> receive from their fathers. Failing to receive a father's love in the home, a young girl may turn to the streets, looking to appease that longing, which they find in the arms of various boys. Such a girl may become promiscuous, jumping (or being passed) from boy to boy, hoping that by giving herself—physically; it will fill the void in her heart. She may think, *"He will love me because I am giving him my body!"* but she could not be more wrong! Most (sexually active) boys have learned to 'hit and run'. Sadly, such a girl may be labeled as a "whore". She may become a target for other boys wanting sex—once it gets out that the first boy has conquered. She may only hear from that partner when he desires to have sex with her again.

Commercial:

Some girls/women (plagued by feelings of rejection) intentionally become pregnant in hope that having a baby will fulfill their desire for someone to love them unconditionally. The painful truth is that once the baby begins to walk and talk, some such mothers lose interest in their child; who is no longer a helpless "doll baby". The teen mother then realizes that she is not equipped to handle the responsibility of raising a child. Being self-centered, many (not all) moms attempt to take back their lives; seeking fun and thus fail to raise their children.

Having a baby only temporarily filled the void—the desire for love. Many young mothers pick up where they left off, searching for someone to love (take care of) them. Now that she has a child, it may become more difficult to find (true) love. Still not knowing what to look for in a man, a teen mother may entertain and have sexual relationships with numerous partners (over time). During her search, she may become pregnant again and then again, (the cycle repeats)!

Some mothers become desperate (whether they admit it or not). Their biological clock is ticking. They are older now; many have yet to be married. They have children now, all growing and needing attention. They may all have different fathers and none of those fathers may be interacting in the children's daily lives. Going back to the beginning, not many males want to raise someone else's children. However, these same males have no problem playing nice until they can have sex with the mother. (Remember the example of the hyenas at the beginning of the chapter?)

Returning to my original thought:

If you are a female (of any age) reading this, you should know that you are worth so much more than (being) a whore, prostitute or booty call. You are priceless and very precious! True love is not found in sex! It is found in a deep connection and relationship with your father and then, when you are older, with your husband!

Sadly, the day will (and has) come for many of our young boys and girls when their mothers will say, *"Sit down,* [Larry, Mike or Rhonda—whatever your name may be], *I need to tell you something. You know, your father is not dead..."* or *"Your father is not the man I told you. He's not the man you know...* Or *"Your father and I had a one-night stand, and I never saw him again. When I found out I was pregnant . . ."* Or (in Jerry Springer or Maury Povich style) *"I really don't know who your father is..."*

This is devastating to a child (no matter how old)! This scenario is played out increasingly with this generation and extends to those that will follow after.

And we wonder why our children are angry and rebellious.

A growing number of our youth are hurt, embittered and (increasingly) out of control! If we looked deeply into their lives to understand why they behave as they do, we would find that a major factor in their behavior stems from the lack of a strong fatherly presence and relationship in their lives. If this breakdown is not corrected and the wounds healed, they will carry these ill feelings into every relationship, adding yet another revolution to the vicious cycle.

Hurt people—hurt people (as the saying goes).

This author is in no way ignorant to the world of today. Because of the overwhelming influences bombarding our youth, households with both parents—doing everything they should do—are finding it hard to raise sensible, respectful and productive children. It is becoming an uphill battle! If you are a parent doing all you can, hang in there! Keep doing all that you know to do. You may be rewarded for your efforts in the end! Teach a child according to what's right, and although they may go astray, they will remember the correct way and (hopefully) return to it!

What do you think would happen when a woman (who was raised without a father) enters into a relationship with a frustrated man (who also was fatherless)?

One should expect conflicts! If the woman is aggressive, she will become frustrated with her husband's (seemingly) lack of motivation, neither understanding nor considering that this man has had no training or guidance from his father. Such a man may be stuck, unable to move forward, because of his lack of knowledge and resources. What such a man has learned might have been illegal. All of his knowledge may be of scamming, hustling and getting over. Perhaps he has his high school diploma or GED—yet his education is not enough to get a good-paying job (or enough to appease his woman) especially in today's economy.

Many violent episodes occur when a frustrated woman confronts a frustrated man. The woman lacks understanding of her man's inadequacies, and the man is unable or unwilling to communicate his problems. In the same instance, the man lacks understanding of his wife's position. She may have never met a "real man" and therefore, may have chosen him because she saw that he had potential. *"I can change him,"* she says to herself. *"I can make (mold) him into the man he could be,"* she tells herself and she enters into the relationship with the mind-set that *she* is going to build or create the *perfect* "man". (Remember, she has little if any knowledge of how a real man behaves, his motivations or how he thinks). Therefore, she will become frustrated. Yet in her arrogance, will she fails to realize that no matter what she says—or does, no one can make another person—change. The person has to want to change. Heck! We can't even change ourselves without help!

In this same manner, the man that arrogantly thinks he can mold his woman into the image of his choosing may employ such tactics as *fear* (there's that word again), abuse and deceptive mind games; all of which will eventually backfire, leaving him in a very humble state.

In all fairness, we must also factor in each of their previous experiences regarding relationships. What baggage did *she* bring into the present relationship? How have her dealings with other men contributed to her perception of men as a whole? Has her experiences left her with bitterness and distrust from a cheating husband or lover; unresolved hurts and fears? What baggage has he brought into the relationship (insecurities, distrust, anger, violence)?

Often, when a (frustrated) woman is attempting to encourage or motivate her man, she uses an aggressive, disrespectful tone. Because she lacks understanding, she shows very little regard for his feelings. She fails to understand that her man is greatly affected by this and receives it as a direct attack; stabbing at his manhood.

News Flash: Neither men nor women like to be spoken to in a disrespectful tone of voice! No one *likes* to be disrespected.

In reaction to her harsh words, the man becomes defensive. After all, most women's perception of men is that a "man" is hard at all times—so her dealings with him will reflect how she perceives a 'real man'.

(It's funny). In one instance, such women want a hard, macho man—yet they desire their man to be sensitive and affectionate toward them. However, such women lack the ability to show the sensitivity and understanding that they so desperately crave from their man.

The relationship suffers! The frustrated woman withdraws from her man. She withholds herself physically, not wanting to be touched; anger bubbling up within her (just below the surface). The man is met with coldness (in speech and actions) whenever they come in contact. Using street terminology, she is no longer *"feeling"* him.

In turn, the man, sensing that his woman has lost respect for him, loses self-confidence. He starts to second guess himself. He may attempt to make things right; buying things or doing tasks and apologizing (repeatedly) hoping that he will win his woman's heart and respect again. However, if his spouse/woman remains unmoved by his efforts, he too will shut down. When a man shuts down, he stops speaking, interacting and may stop doing anything productive. At this point the woman has killed his *spirit*. She confronts; he withdraws—deeper. Such a relationship is in desperate trouble! Eventually, the man begins to find other things to occupy his time. He may spend less and less time at home. Because he has been wounded and his self-esteem has hit bottom, he may go someplace where he *feels* accepted and respected. (At this point, it is very easy for such a man to sink into depression, begin to abuse drugs/alcohol, lash out physically or enter into an affair. The relationship between such couples may *never* recover and could—die).

On the other hand, the man (who has never witnessed the tender interactions between his father and mother), will most likely speak to his wife as if she were a pet. His words: demands, criticisms and overall treatment of his woman, may crush her spirit and cause her to sink into depression and to have low self-esteem. She may begin overeating, use drugs/alcohol, have emotional breakdowns, battle with suicide and she too may stray into the arms of another. Such a man does not understand his wife's needs beyond security. She desires conversation, intimacy and encouragement. Such men tend to look at their woman as an object or possession; not as a partner and friend. Man of this nature tends to have no problem hitting (abusing) his woman.

Great is the need for our fathers!

Great is the need for real men to fill the gaps in the lives of our children (which will affect their relationships in the future)!

Some Parting Thoughts about Fathers

A father produces that which is 'good' and draws out goodness from whom and/or what he cares for!

The responsibility of a man/father is awesome yet very rewarding!

Don't let your environment steal your manhood.

Those of us who are without fathers may in fact already know of a man who is father like; he may be our coach, teacher, uncle or minister. Connect with that man if you can!

A father's work is often unnoticed. He's often taken for granted. He's usually exhausted and worn but the results of his labor can be seen in the personalities, behavior, strength, unity and happiness of his family!

There is one Father who has cared for us, loved us and desires a relationship with us all!

Fathers, do not provoke your children to anger, but bring them up in the discipline and instruction of the Lord. (Ephesians 6:4)

Train up a child in the way he should go, Even when he is old he will not depart from it. Proverbs 22:6

Fathers, do not exasperate your children, so that they will not lose heart. (Colossians 3:21)
Listen to your father who begot you, and do not despise your mother when she is old. (Proverbs 23:22)

A good man leaves an inheritance to his children, And the wealth of the sinner is stored up for the righteous. Proverbs 13:22)

Messages in the

Music

I. L. Jackson

Messages in the Music

Before we begin our discussion of music, this author feels it necessary to state that this author is in no way attempting to dictate what a person should or should not listen to. This author's attempt is to give warning about the power and effects of music. It is ultimately your decision what and whom you choose to listen to.

What is music?

Music is organized sounds or tones fitted together in such a way that it creates a melodious, harmonious or rhythmic flow.

Music is (also) a mood setter and enhancer. Music has the power to set or get us to feel a certain way as well as strengthening what we are already feeling.

- Sad or depressed
- Romantic or sexual
- Anger or rage, etc.
- Music can make us feel a certain way that we did not feel previously!
- Happy
- Sad
- Mellow or peaceful
- Victorious and inspired

Music is powerful, hypnotic, affecting us at our core. Music goes straight to our hearts!

What are lyrics?

Lyrics are the words that are put to music.

Lyrics influence our thinking by transmitting ideas, painting pictures of stories and situations, expressing feelings and so on.

When words are added to music, it becomes a double-edged sword or double-barreled shotgun!

- Repetitious lyrics become lodged in the mind, affecting the way we think about the subject matter of the song (played long enough, we become more accepting of what we hear though we may have disagreed at first). This is extremely dangerous!
- Lyrics ride the music (melody or beat) straight to the heart (where we make *all* of our decisions).

Note: *The heart is the place where we truly know something. We do not say, "I know that song by head." We say, "I know that song by heart!" Furthermore, although our brains may present us with a choice of actions, it is the heart that makes the final decision to move! One has not truly made a decision until one takes action!*

Why does the thug or macho man avoid listening to wimpy love songs (in public)?

Because a love song would melt his heart and he would do anything to avoid being seen as weak in any way!

Why are young girls having babies at an ever-increasing rate?

One contributing factor is that most girls (and most women) give full vent to their emotions.

Females tend to behave according to what they feel. If they are angry, they give themselves totally to that anger! If they are depressed or worried, they give themselves totally (mind/spirit and body) to depression or anxiety. Therefore, women have far more emotional breakdowns, headaches and a higher suicide rate than men. (If a young girl feels that she is in love, that feeling consumes her totally!)

A growing number of love songs have explicit lyrics. These lyrics hit right in the center of a female's emotions. The imagery, the firm ruggedness of the man in the video, his voice (as smooth as silk), the way he moves (*Sigh . . .*) the seductive music, the enticing lyrics… (Ooh yeah)! *Gotcha!*

(We'll continue to explore this scenario a little later.)

Why are so many young men (and now women) caught up in the drug game, in violence and the like?

Could it be that our youth are constantly hearing drugs, sex and violence glorified in the music and videos they watch (among other things)?

As we have learned previously, the subject matter of the songs is repeated (rehearsed) in their minds; filling their hearts. The lyrics are like hypnotic suggestions that are activated when the person is faced with that particular situation.

Will they resist or will they give in to the suggestions that were laced within the music?

This will be determined by their level of self-esteem, their ability to resist peer pressure, the strength of their values and their understanding of consequences!

Music is so powerful! Music can heal the heart and eases the mind, yet (more and more) it disrupts and corrupts. This should not be!

Note: *Music has the ability to tie all races, economic backgrounds and societies together! Check out the concert halls and stadiums! Only at these venues do we truly find the complete abandonment of racial hatred, economic status, his or her opinions, etc. Why is this? Because there is something about music that binds all peoples! Even at sporting events, you have division; one side against another, one group of fans for one team, another group of fans for the opposing team. Only at concerts do you see every one (of differing races and religions) gathering and cheering for the same reason—to enjoy the music! Sadly, even the church continues to have racial separation.*

If only there was more music that uplifted the next man or woman and that was played to promote good and positive ideals; songs that might say:

- Together as a family or community, we can make it!
- We need each other, my brother!
- I love you, my sisters (men's anthem to women)

- You can still lean on me!
- Be there for me, and I'll be there for you!
- Here, let me help you!

(Corny, idealistic, lame, weak, whack—whatever, I'm wit' it!) This is why many are increasingly turning their ear to inspirational or gospel music. Such music ministers to their pain, loneliness, depression or hurt and offers—hope!

Know this! Whatever is in an individual's heart that is what he or she is likely to do!

- Have sex
- Commit acts of violence
- Become angry or hateful
- Feel happiness or joy
- Feel depressed or suicidal
- Commit murder

Did you know that our hearts sing?

Have you ever awakened out of a sound sleep and heard a song playing in your head, or have you found yourself singing some catchy tune you've heard somewhere and even when you're relaxing, thinking or doing hard work, you can still hear it?

The heart *"sings"* the condition of our spirits!

- A broken heart (spirit) sings sad songs or a song of encouragement
- A bitter, angry heart sings songs of violence and hate
- A happy heart sings songs of joy (Thus, when we see someone singing joyfully, we say, "You're in good 'spirits!'")

Think about it!

What are we listening to?

- Love songs or lust songs

- Songs of hate rage and rebellion
- Songs of hope and encouragement

Here's a thought:

A young girl is listening to the radio when a song is played. This new song is hot! The girl calls her best friend and tells her about this new jam. Both girls eagerly search for the song and if they are able—they download it. Over and over again, these young ladies start, stop, and replay. They may even write down the lyrics so that they can learn the words.

Let's say that this is a love song whose lyrics explicitly describe a sexual act. What is happening to these two girls? They are being programmed, actually brainwashed or hypnotized, desiring to have sex! The evidence of this can be seen in the humorous conversations that these girls may have with the recording artist's poster, hanging on the wall of their bedroom (fantasizing about having a relationship with that person)!

Seriously, these young ladies may be easily coaxed into having sex because they have already done it in their hearts and imagined it in their minds (thanks to this new song)! These girls would be in even bigger trouble if one of them were to meet a boy who looks like or can sing like her favorite artist! She will most likely become a victim of "the game" and a teen mom!

(In this same manner, both boys and girls may be enticed into using and selling drugs and becoming violent!)

Here's another example of music's appeal and influence:

Suppose you were to walk into a room filled with teenagers all awaiting an acclaimed speaker to expound. The speaker is introduced! As soon as he/she steps to the podium, he/she begins to describe what he/she is currently wearing and how much money is in his or her pockets. "Hello! First, I'd like to call everyone's attention to my jacket; it's 100 percent Italian silk! Do you see my shirt? It cost me . . . . ! My pants or skirt is . . . ! Plus, check out my watch! It's such and such..! And my socks . . . !" This continues for about five minutes! Then, as suddenly as this person began speaking, he or she stops and sits down. This, by the way, is not a fashion show!

Open your eyes…Face the truth!

What would be your thoughts if you were sitting in this room at that time? Some might say, "Why is he or she telling us this? We don't care!" Others might say, "Shut up"—or worse! Some may get up and leave. Still others might think to themselves, "If I were that type, I'd rob that so and so!" The point I'm attempting to make here is that most of us wouldn't care in the least about this person's clothing (though they may be quite nice)! "OK! He or she looks good, but he or she doesn't have to brag though!"

Now, if this same person was to walk into the same room saying the very same things, this time in the form of a rap or poem, the overall reaction in the room would be quite different. In fact, the speaker may receive applause and high fives!

Think about it!

What was so different?

It was the same message!

Why was the rap accepted and the speech rejected?

It was the delivery! The message sounded better because it was packaged in such a way that it grabbed their attention and kept them interested.

Many destructive thoughts and messages are transmitted in this way. They are accepted because they are relayed in the form of a song, hidden within the lyrics and a catchy beat or melody!

Music (lyrics) reflects the spiritual condition of the person who wrote it.

From gospel to acid rock, rap to country western, whatever the artist was feeling or doing (drugs/alcohol) comes through in the music (lyrics)! This causes one to think as they think and to feel as they feel (for at least four minutes or so). If one were to replay a certain song, what would one be taking into his heart (spirit)?

- Braggadocios posturing
- Drugged or drunken ramblings

- Sexual and lust-filled fantasies
- Hateful, violent, murderous threats
- Rebellious and defiant outbursts
- Social commentary, idealism
- Love and affection
- Godly praise and worship

The symptoms of a sick generation can be found in the lyrics of its music!

In other words, our youth are a direct reflection of the music they listen to. (You are what you eat, so to speak)!

What is a curse?

A curse is a (spoken) wish of hurt or harm over someone.

Words have power (to build or destroy, to encourage or discourage, to praise/speak highly of or to slander/murder with the tongue!)

- Verbal abuse/violence (which affects one's emotions and mentality) can be far worse than physical violence! Most physical injuries will heal in a matter of weeks but emotional wounds cannot be healed without help (some persons never recover)!
- We can literally kill one's reputation and spirit with our words! (If one's spirit dies, he/she may still exist but he/she (his or her personality or fire, who he/she really is) is no longer living!

Everything started with words and all things will end with words!

- Dad and Mom met and spoke to each other (even if they used social media or sign language)
- Things we have or desire, we ask for or talk about them
- We understand that wars are started and ended with words
- Ideas, plans, etc. come to pass through words

If it has not been spoken aloud (or written), it does not exist!

An idea or thought that is never spoken, written down or acted upon only exists in the mind of the one who came up with it. It does not exist to anyone else.

If an idea or thought has been shared with others, it exists because now others share or understand what is on a person's mind. There is now something that others can grasp and build upon.

A destructive word (curse) destroys and tears down (another person or persons).

- *"I hate you!"*
- *"Dummy! You're so stupid!"*
- *"That will never work!"*
- *"You're not built like that," "You can't do that," "You're incapable of doing or achieving that"*
- *"You suck!"*
- *"Give it up! You're never going to be…!"*

A positive word encourages and builds up (one's self-esteem)!

- *"I love you!"*
- *"You can do it! If you work hard at it, you can do anything!"*
- *"That looks great!"*
- *"Keep it up! You're doing great!"*

Words taken into one's heart and 'believed' will produce thoughts and actions based on those words! (A child that is continually called *stupid* will most likely believe and act *stupidly*.)

We *can* reject or accept words (and thoughts)! However, we cannot reject a thing (person or place) if we continue to listen to or hang around (with) it!

Since our subject here is music, we must understand that listening to certain types continually and repeatedly will begin to shape our thoughts (this is especially dangerous in the case of small children).

Music's influence (with the help of videos):

128

- Can turn good boys into players, thugs and 'gangstas'
- Can turn good girls into *"ride or die"* chicks, video hoes, b@*#, etc.
- Has (very) young girls performing sexual dances (twerking, winding and grinding—backing it up and touching their toes, or—if you're a little older—perculatin', droppin' down—getting' their eagle on, etc.)
- Promotes and glamorizes premarital sex, blunt smoking, drug dealing and usage, cheating (adultery), orgies, etc.

Sex, drugs and violence run rampant through the music!

Sex, drugs, rebellion and anger—sells!

Wholesome, insightful, beautiful music (for the most part) lacks the financial backing, packaging, glitz and glamour that the other more risqué music has!

We must change our minds! We must change our way of thinking!

People are going to do what they want to do but understand that immorality should not be advertised as if it were something that should be grasped or desired. Unfortunately, however, this is the state of today's society.

Know this! Each generation has and will become increasingly worse because we are constantly bombarded with advertisements, movies, radio, social media posts/videos and television programs that promote and support low moral conduct and foul behavior.

Do you want to know what's on the minds of today's youth? Listen to what they listen to for an hour or two!

Through the advances in technology; internet, smart phones and the ever increasing number of social networks, our youth are exposed to more and more knowledge at earlier ages. They are smarter than we adults and are more twisted in their thinking; and it is because of what we have exposed them to. They have great knowledge without understanding (wisdom)!

Today's generation is doing the "dirt" that the previous generation did yet they are doing it younger, in greater amounts and frequency! (I am speaking of sex, drugs, corruption, violence—even murder.)

Open your eyes…Face the truth!

Truly, knowledge without wisdom can be deadly!

It leads to the following:
- Arrogance, self-righteousness
- Resentment and bitterness
- Ruthlessness
- Rebellion
- Immorality

(All of which are rapidly increasing)

There is no restraint!

There are many messages woven within music (some positive, others negative). One of the negative messages sent through the music is that which separates and pits males and females at odds.

Some of the messages sent to males:

- Girls are hoes (whores). They aren't worthy of respect. These…aren't loyal"—so treat them poorly! Don't love 'em!
- Women are gold diggers. They (women in general) will only love you as long as the money's coming in.
- Sleep with as many females as you can—player!
- If you want to get the girls, you've got to have money, a nice car and some "bling" (diamonds).
- It's rare but you might find a "ride or die" chick (a girl who will help her man steal, bag up drugs, etc.), so hold on to that one! But understand that she cannot be fully trusted.
- Women are like cigarettes, smoke 'em, toss 'em—spark up another one. Or like a joint (marijuana), take a hit and pass her to your boy!
- Play on player, get yours!

Some messages sent to females:

- If he can't pay my bills, he gets no play (no conversation, phone number and definitely not sex)!

- Don't mess with a "scrub" (a man without a lot of money; still lives with his mother and doesn't have his own car).
- Dressing like a video vixen is cool! It gets the attention of the guys who have money!
- Showing off your body or "giving it up" is the way to obtain the things you want. "You've got to use what you have to get what you want!"
- Play the game; after all, men have been doing it to (women) for years!

These are the messages that are sent to our youth (both males and females). Hopefully, these examples are enough to prove my point!

We must wake up! We must make people aware of what's being pumped into the ears of our youth—and we adults are just as caught up.

When the music that is made dwells on the negative; the way things are (bad experiences, drugs, poverty, abuse, hate, etc.), listeners will accept and repeat what they have heard. The artists' words will form (for many) their worldview. Things shall remain as they have always been or they will get worse. Yet if more music were to be made expressing what could be, change will begin because listeners will repeat what they have heard and their actions will reflect those ideals!

One of this author's favorite songs is *"the Message"* by Grandmaster Flash and the Furious Five. The song spoke about a person dealing with the struggle of living in the 'ghetto'. The chorus of the song goes *"Don't push me 'cause I'm close to the edge. I'm trying not to lose my head... It's like a jungle sometimes. It makes me wonder how I keep from going under..."* This song was an anthem and it was a warning! It was a pivotal point in rap music akin to Marvin Gaye's classic album "What's Going on?" However, many rappers that followed did not catch "the message" (no pun intended). Attempting to capture the reality and emotion of this song, other rappers have told their realities or what they have claimed to be their 'truth'—only to glamorize a lifestyle that was _never_ theirs. They have created fantasies in order to sell records. Songs like "the Message" are cries of social awareness, saying *"Look people, we are hurting and struggling over here..."* If you ever get a chance to listen to the song, you will see that the rappers have not fallen into the things that are all around... they are yet holding on—still doing what's right)!

Open your eyes…Face the truth!

The artists' words become reality for many!

Singers, rappers and movie stars have no idea of the great power they possess, or perhaps they do! Their influence is tremendous! (Consider this.) Millions of people (worldwide) tune in daily to listen to what these people have to say. We download their albums or buy their CDs. We search the web, reading articles about our favorite artists; we follow their words on social networks listen to their interviews on BET, MTV, etc. We run to the stores to buy the same outfits we saw them wearing in their videos, so on and so on. Yet many of these influential people will firmly deny that they are role models.

Countless others have stories to tell as well yet most will never have the opportunities that these stars have to voice their opinion before millions of others! So while these artists still have an audience, prayerfully they will give them something positive to listen to and memorize! To borrow a phrase from the movie *Spiderman, "With great power comes great responsibility,"* and we will give an account for what we have done with our gifts and talents (whether good or evil). Believe that!

Short-Term Solutions

- Consider what we watch and listen to in the presence of our children.
- Do not allow them to watch or listen to programs and songs that promote negative messages.
- Make sure programming is appropriate to their age.
- Use parental controls on computers and other devices to restrict unwanted websites on the Internet and also cable channels
- Do your homework! Watch and listen to material before presenting it to your children.
- Make it a point to watch and listen to programs and songs with your children. Discuss the material (what are the children thinking, feeling, etc.).

Below is a nursery-rhyme-styled checklist that will help you determine the theme of those programs and songs that we are listening to. Memorizing this simple rhyme (though it may seem childish) will assist you in getting to the root of what's really being said in every area of your life! (It has helped me to see the truth behind many things, much of which you are reading right now!)

I. L. Jackson

What's the message? Is it true? Is it good for me and you?
*(Taken from the Here's Looking at You 2000 drug and alcohol curriculum)

We <u>MUST</u> reject what goes against good morals. Turn away, turn it off or leave.

Once again, this author is well aware that people are going to do what they want to do, however:

- Parents, (please) stop allowing your children to listen to music having explicit lyrical content
- Stop taking them with you to R-rated movies. (*Would you have sex in the room with your children watching?* Please say no. Please—say NO!)

Parents (myself included); our children are listening to the same things as us (especially in most African American households). What we allow them to listen to and to watch will contribute to the way they will think, accept and behave in the future!

Children begin to rebel when they realize that we are playing the hypocrite, doing and saying the very things that we tell them are wrong!

This tells our children that:

- "It must be OK!" Dad and Mom are watching and listening to it. (Have you ever seen the commercial when the Dad confronts his son about smoking marijuana and the son blurts out, "I learned it by watching you Dad!"?)
- "They're hypocrites!"
- "Since they're doing it [when they are not around], so will I!"

We all stumble here but we must continue to work on it. It takes time, courage and discipline but you (and I) can do it!

Change does not happen overnight. Change happens over time!

Open your eyes...Face the truth!

Speaking to one another with psalms, hymns, and songs from the Spirit. Sing and make music from the heart to the Lord, (Ephesians 5:19)

He says, "I will declare your name to my brothers and sisters; in the assembly I will sing your praises." (Hebrew 2:12)

My lips will shout for joy when I sing praise to you—whom you have delivered. (Psalm 71:23)

I. L. Jackson

Let me tell you what I saw...

This rhyme is for the sake of others, my sisters & my brothers
Not to lift self, not to brag about my wealth.
My lyrics are 'life giving'. Restoring the blind's visions,
(Whose) minds are lock, chained, oppressed by the system.
I've been given keys to free 'peeps' from prisons!
I warn youth—against making bad decisions,
How people on evil missions have made plans to trick 'em—
Even their parents fall victim! (Man Listen...)
Evil's on every side! Through sex, drugs and violence we're committing suicide!
And who can hide? What's coming through our ears and eyes?
Is there any surprise, homicide is on a rise?
Now who am I? I'm like a "watchman" on the wall.
I've stared into darkness—let me tell you what I saw!
It's bugged... brothers living to sell drugs, dying to be thugs...
Hateful, without love! Fools are breeding ...
They multiply like roaches! They stop dead in their tracks...
When the "light of truth" exposes (them completely and so neatly)!
We're like an endangered species, living' foul like feces, rotten and stinking...
(Man) we've got to change our thinking!
Peep these videos; convince girls to shed their clothes,
Bare bodies all exposed—a generation of "hoes"!
Brothers give these girls babies, but won't give them their name...
Mad 'cause their dads left them—now they're doing the same!
And it's a shame—but it's a game, I'm afraid...
It's a game without winners! Every player will get played!
Someone lies and bullets fly! Murders and suicides...
Someone else turns to drugs and O.D's chasing a high!
Now a family's cries—reach up past the sky...
As a mother screams *"Why did my baby have to die?"*
Heaven heavily sighs; her pain intensified in the heart of the "Most High"!
(But) who runs to God's side? Who wipes tears from God's eyes...?
When children die before their time...
Realize—God cries!

Written by: I. L. Jackson

Our teacher—the media!

(Television, radio, social media, etc.)

Our Teacher--the media!
(Television, radio, social media, etc.)

(Once again, this author feels that it is necessary to state that I am not attempting to rain on anyone's parade and hinder them from watching what they find enjoyable. Do you! This author is merely attempting to enlighten you on how music and now (in this chapter), the media (television, radio, social media, etc.) has a way of affecting our way of thinking, our worldview and even our behavior! I pray that you will carefully consider the things written in these chapters.)

Television and social media are teachers! Don't get it twisted!

If you watch television, you are being taught something:

- News and weather (current events, sports, world news)
- PBS (science, nature, art, culture, history, child development and education)
- Soap operas (sex, adultery, backstabbing, greed, lust, lies and deception)
- Talk shows (gossip, foul language, betrayal, adultery, alternative lifestyles, human interest)
- Sitcoms (sex, drugs, alternative lifestyles, rebellion (disrespect toward parents and authority, rudeness, backstabbing, greed, foul language and distrust)
- Wrestling (violence, foul language, disrespect and violence toward women, betrayals)
- High impact/reality shows (greed, lust, casual sex, frequent fighting and bickering, backstabbing, distrust, stepping over and on others to get what is "mine," anti-teamwork—me, me, me, survival of the fittest)
- Cartoons (humor, slapstick, rebellion, fantasy, magic, (interest in) witchcraft, violence, social responsibility, morals, etc.)
- Game shows (knowledge of various things, gambling, greed, competition, etc.)
- Real TV (real-life situations, caught in the act, danger, violence, explosions, accidents, etc.)

- Cable and direct television broadcasts everything under the sun. Anything that sparks your interest can be found by scrolling through the menu.

The same things listed above are presently being spread through social media—but at a faster rate! News of all kinds, that was once seen only at certain times and or by certain people at a time is now spread at the blink of an eye via posts of videos, texts, blogging, etc.

There is no doubt media is a teacher. Television is a teacher. Depending on what an individual watches, he/she may be learning many things, both good and bad at the same time. For instance on a reality show, one might learn that using teamwork is a great way for a group of people to reach a common goal. Yet when the opportunity presents itself, it may be necessary to backstab and or deceive others to achieve one's individual goal. Or someone might learn that he should not beat up on women—but if it's on wrestling, it's ok!

How is a virus spread? What is an epidemic?

A virus is spread when the carrier of the virus comes into contact with others (through breath, touch or through being left on a surface by someone who is a carrier).

*epidemic- is a fast spreading disease, an outbreak of a disease that spreads more quickly and more extensively among a group of people than would normally be expected (Encarta Dictionary: English (North America)

There is now another widespread epidemic that is plaguing us all; and it is coming via TV, video games, music, the Internet/social media.

We may think they're just entertainment—but we are constantly being bombarded with the thoughts, views, opinions and moral ideals of others. Consequently, today, the expression "alternative" is used to justify inordinate behavior, rebellion, etc.

We accept a lot of moral junk because it comes through the media: TV, radio, and via the social networks.

"Well, why don't you turn the channel, the station—or don't go on those networks?" You might ask.

The problem is that wholesome or family TV, radio and whatever—lacks the financial backing and power that the more edgy programming has. Edgy is more exciting! Sex sells!

- Because of less funding, family "programming" is rare.
- Because of mass appeal, along with greater financial backing, edgy—less wholesome "programming" can continue to excite and dazzle with big budget productions (explosions, fancy cars, clothes and special effects).

They feed us "eye candy"! We eat it up and ask for more!

What does it mean to be brainwashed?

Brainwashing is the act of imposing beliefs on somebody by utilizing forceful methods;

What is hypnosis?

Hypnosis is an artificially induced condition- a condition that can be induced in people, in which they can respond to questions and are very susceptible to suggestions from the hypnotist (Encarta Dictionary: English (North America)

The media is a powerful tool used to influence people on a mass scale to reject what they know or believe—and accept whatsoever is told to them.
It's as simple as running a fast-food or soda commercial in front of a person over and over again. The person may not be hungry or thirsty but what is shown looks so good he/she has to have one for him/her *'self'*. One might not run out and buy today—but when the opportunity presents itself, it's on!

Maybe it's not food! Maybe it's:

- A car
- Clothing or jewelry
- A toy or game

Open your eyes…Face the truth!

- A place (a vacation spot or theme park)

We all are being brainwashed/hypnotized by something!

Sex, drugs and violence are all advertised. They are displayed and taught on TV, radio, the internet and all other forms of media.

People are in love with the risqué. (That is why the soap operas, Basketball Wives, Real house Wives… and the like are so popular! There is something in us that draws us to drama and smut.) And, as far as drugs are concerned, as an experiment, count how many drug commercials you see if you're watching prime time TV tonight.

We *are* being *programmed* by television, radio and other "media"!

What does programming mean?

*program-1. A broadcast 2. Plan of action; for achieving something

A program is a list of data or information that outlines the desired course of actions for a plan to be accomplished. - *Encarta Dictionary*

A computer is given a program (known as software or an "app" [application]). The computer follows those things laid out by that particular program or app. If the computer is asked to do something that is not in the program or plan (software), it simply cannot. It will say something like, *"This computer has done something illegally, you must do…"* The illegal procedure might cause the computer to 'crash'! The only thing one can do in such an instance is to turn the computer of and restart it! (I'm speaking in terms of computers and of our minds).

In the same manner, we are receiving thoughts, points of view and opinions that are *programming* us to think according to what we've been watching or listening to. This can be quite dangerous.

Example: A young child is introduced to pornography. He or she then goes to school and behaves according to the *'program'* he or she has been exposed to.

140

*(This *'programming'* works the same for drugs, anger and violence, etc.—and positive things as well).

What happens next? Well, like the computer, we perform according to our *programming*. We function according to what is or has been instilled in us. Like computers, we are unable to perform outside of what we have been *programmed* to think. Certain actions and ways of thinking are just foreign to us.

There is a movie called *'The Matrix'* that is not too far from the truth! Our minds are being imprisoned by negative programming and set on a course to self-destruct!

Advertisement is another word for brainwashing/hypnotism—or programming. The single goal of advertising is to convince people that they cannot live without certain products—*even if they neither need nor want it*. There are good products and there are bad ones.

One goal of advertisers is to make even the most deadly products attractive—a must-have!

- Cigarettes (i.e. "cancer sticks")
- Malt liquor
- Questionable drugs (weight loss, etc.) with their many side effects

Brainwashing = Trends and Fads!

Trends and fads are "mindsets"—ways of thinking that say:
- *"I accept this,"*
- *"I desire this,"*
- *"This is in!"* or
- *"That is played out—or "that's out of style"*

"Media" (Television, radio, and now social networks, movies, etc.,) is the vehicle used to spread (desired) social ideals.

Advertising and marketing are other names for "propaganda".

Open your eyes…Face the truth!

Propaganda- 1. information put out by an organization or government to promote a policy, idea, or cause 2. deceptive or distorted information that is systematically spread

"Seeing—is believing" for most of us! Many people have adopted this attitude. *"If I can see it, then I'll know that it is true,"* and *"I've got to see it in order to understand it."* (You may be asking yourself, *"What is this author saying?"*)

Most of us learn more by *"seeing"* than by (just) hearing.

What are we learning through what we see?

For instance, a close examination of anime (Japanese animation) to which many have an outgoing love affair reveals the following:

- Advances in technology
- Vivid expressions of the imagination
- Philosophy (various beliefs, codes of conduct)
- Graphic displays of violence, blood and gore, ruthless murder, sorcery, witchcraft, satanic themes (demons and monsters) and (sometimes) pornography

❖ Also, there is the Exploitation of the female body, (even young girls)

(Not everything is negative. However, recently there has been an upsurge of magic, witchcraft, sorcery and satanic content on TV and in movies!)

Such material is now being viewed on a daily basis. The extended viewing of such programming may result in:

- The desire for supernatural power
- Satan worship, spiritual dealings (séances, tarot and psychic)
- The practice of witchcraft and black magic (this is very real)
- The formation of or membership in the occult
- Violence (potential harm and injury to one's self and others)
- Suicide and homicide

Satan worship and witchcraft are very real!

Why do we act the way we do?

Consider this:

- Watching karate and Kung-Fu movies inspire or motivate us to act or play like we know Kung-Fu!
- Watching wrestling makes us want to wrestle (I know that I am not the only person to watch wrestling, get so excited that during the commercials, I'd turn to my brother, even to my children, and begin to flip them around the room!)
- Watching pornography makes us want to have sex!
- Watching gangster flicks makes us want to be gangsters! (Ask any drug dealer, "What's your favorite movie?" you can bet that such movies as: *Scar Face, The King of New York, The God Father, State Property—and "American Gangster"* would be at the top of their lists!

The more we expose ourselves to such programs (sex, violence, hatred, etc.), the more we are likely to act out what we've been watching or learning.

We are constantly being bombarded by thoughts from others, trying to convince us that *their* way is the correct way—or that we need what they are offering:

- Family and friends
- Boyfriends/girlfriends
- Music (singers, rappers, and musicians)
- Clothing designers
- Restaurants
- Car companies, etc.

Everyone is trying to get us to think and/or act in a certain way—the way they would like us to think (whether on TV, radio, social media, in person, in conversations, in books, etc.). Therefore, it is very, very important that we pay close attention to what we watch and listen to.

Open your eyes…Face the truth!

Has anyone else noticed the sudden upsurge of homosexual programming on prime time (the hours that target our youth and family)? Is this the new trend? What is really being said? Now look at the growing number of same sex marriages and the increase of homosexual activity throughout our nation and especially amongst our youth!

Free your mind!

Here (again) is a saying that works very well when dealing with situations involving decision making and that helps free your mind from falling into traps.

What's the message? Is it true? Is it good for me and you?
(Taken from Here's Looking at You 2000, a drug education curriculum 7th grade tub).

Turn away my eyes from looking at vanity, and revive me in Your ways. (Psalm 119:37)

Let your eyes look directly ahead and let your gaze be fixed straight in front of you. (Proverbs 4:25)

He who walks righteously and speaks with sincerity. who despises the gain of oppressions; who shakes his hands, lest they hold a bribe, who stops his ears from hearing of bloodshed and shut his eyes from looking on evil, he will dwell on the heights; his place of defense will be the fortresses of rocks; his bread will be given him; his water will be sure. Isaiah (33:15-16 ESV)

They don't know... (What I see!) Written by: I. L. Jackson

(They don't know... what I see! They don't know...what I see!)

I'm talking about the youth, the schools
...the scholar—the fool!
(Yo!) Knowledge is power and school is cool!
The Math, the English, the History, the Science...
The students, rebellious, defiant and violent!
The cursing, the cussing, the teasing, the busting...
The hours in classes—and yet learning nothing!
The teachers, the students,
The fighting, the wars...
The quest to be popular, the low test scores!
The principal, the parents, the meetings (no doubt)!
The warnings...
The day they had to kick your tail out!
The days, the weeks, the months, they pass and...
The day of graduation, you're missing in action!

(They don't know... what I see! They don't know...what I see!)

(I'm talking about) the streets, the thugs, the hustling, the drugs...
No peace, no love—just blood. It's bugged...!
The plan, the mission, the capture, the prison,
The time on "lock down" 'cause you just wouldn't listen!
In life there're struggles. In life, there's pain!
At times you'll feel like you're going insane!
The pressure, the stress, the trials, the tests,
The key to success—just press through the mess!
Neglected? Abused? The suffering at home...
Your strength maybe gone...
You're not alone! Hold on!

The victory is coming!
The victory is sure!
The victory is yours...
Endure, Endure...!

The power of words (thoughts)

The Power of Words /Thoughts
("So what'chu saying?")

What is a word?

A word is a spoken or written name; a description given to a person, place, thing, emotion or idea.

A word is used to communicate and express thoughts.

Depending on how words are used, they can be either or good or bad—encourage or tear down according to the *spirit* in which they were spoken or written.

If the *spirit* behind a word or thought is good, it encourages; but if it is an evil *spirit* behind the word, then it is a curse!

Curse—a wish of harm, an evil word either spoken or written.

What is a thought?

- It is an idea, opinion, suggestion, mental activity, reflection.
- Words that form in the mind or enter the mind from an outside source.

Thoughts are much like trees. Like trees, thoughts start small—as seeds.
Trees and thoughts require the right conditions to grow. Both require:

- Fertile soil- Trees cannot grow if the soil in which it is planted is not fertile. Thoughts require the fertile soil of an open mind that is willing to receive it, hold it and nurture it to maturity.

- Water- Tree seeds need water, so do thoughts. Thoughts are "watered" by dwelling on them—repeatedly listening or viewing things that strengthen the original thoughts. Depression, anger, lustful thoughts, etc., are strengthened when we meditate on them.

- Roots- Like tree seeds, thoughts take root. As a tree grows taller, its roots spread and pushes deeper into the ground. The longer a way of thinking is continued, the deeper its roots push into our minds.

- Fruit (reproduction) - Trees bring forth fruit (apples, oranges, acorns, etc.). Likewise, thoughts bring forth *fruit*. The fruit of a thought is behavior, actions, reactions and habits (whether bad or good).

When trees reproduce, forests, woods and groves spring up according to its kind. Therefore, we have entire forests of pine trees, maple, oak, etc. We also have various orchards and such, like apples, oranges, pears, and such!

In order to chop down a huge tree, it must be done in sections. (I speak of a tree that has grown in a place where its falling will cause damage to something we would like to keep.)

- First, certain branches must be sawed off.
- Next, the trunk is cut in sections.
- The stump usually remains (because the roots are tangled and wrapped around pipes or other important fixtures).

The stump is not (always) dead! You must remove the stump at the roots or there may still be life! This author has seen small branches sprout up out of the sides of a tree stump. The roots may still be growing. If left alone, there is a possibility that another tree will be formed.

You must kill the tree at the roots!

In like manner, when we speak of tearing down a *stronghold* (a way of thinking that has grown powerful overtime and has become *deep-rooted*), the root (the initial cause) must be found and dealt with. This will not be an easy task! Moreover, no one has the power to free one's self from a stronghold (heroin addiction, for example). In fact, it is impossible!

Many individuals—from average Joes to movie stars, millionaires and corporate executives—fortunes each year in rehabilitation and therapy! There is no favor or special privileges when it comes to *strongholds*. Having wealth means nothing! Despite their money, their power and/or influence most addicts continue to be plagued by their *demons* (anger, addictions, depression, fears/phobias, disappointments, perversions and hurts. The Betty Ford Clinic, for example, is overflowing with the rich and famous that has (repeatedly) *checked in* because they have had a relapse.

Although therapy helps, it does not completely cure! That is why many individuals (faithfully) attend therapy for years. The "roots" of a stronghold wrap themselves around so many areas of our minds that an individual must literally be taught a new way of thinking (processing) and functioning. As we spoke of in the previous chapter, the malevolent programming (software) of the mind must be dumped and replaced by the *correct* programming. Like a little child, the individual must be trained in the way that he or she *should* go!

But who will do this training?

The psychiatrist or therapist has his or her own life. Would a psychiatrist want to be bogged down with all of his/her patients twenty-four hours a day, seven days a week—as well as function in his/her marriage and be a parent to his/her (own) children? I think not! Furthermore, who has that much money to continue paying their shrinks' hourly rate?

Returning to our comparison of trees and thoughts about the trees; what if the 'stump' remains?

The person recovering from alcoholic and the individual suffering from drug addiction are told that they will <u>never</u> be (completely) freed from their illness. They are told that they must take it one day at a time. This is because the "stump" remains and the roots still have a firm grip on their minds. This means that they (still) have the same mindset! The addiction may have gone into remission; however, it can rear its head at any time. In cases of addiction, the *stronghold* merely retreats and resurfaces in another (more acceptable) form. For example: crack addiction may hide and emerge as drinking, smoking cigarettes and/or overeating. As a side-affect an individual may become highly critical of others and self-righteous.)

What if, like in the example of the trees, the stronghold has already reproduced?

What if an entire forest of destructive thinking has taken over the mind? (Think about it!)

There is only one way that *strongholds* can be eliminated! We will discuss this in a later chapter.

Let's move on!

Bad (negative or destructive) thoughts are like weeds!

Weeds grow in strange places. They grow:

- In the midst of crops
- In gardens
- Out of cement
- In and on abandoned houses (in unoccupied places), etc.

*(Think about it. We are *still* discussing thoughts and our minds).

Weeds strangle other plants, stealing the life from them, stunting their growth (so that whatever is supposed to be growing cannot reach its full potential)!

Destructive and evil thoughts choke and hinder positive thinking, keeping us from seeing, realizing and reaching our full potential, our destinies— our goals.

We must break free from the negative thought patterns (weeds) in our lives and maximize our potential!

Weeds start out as seeds! Negative thoughts start out as seeds!!

The seeds of trees, flowers and weeds are blown by the wind or carried by some animal or insect to various places. Negative and destructive thoughts travel in a similar manner. When someone speaks, their words travel from one's mouth to the ears of those who are able to hear what has been said. What has been said and heard is often repeated to others—and still others. Stories, history, songs (remember our discussion on music?), ideas and even rumors (gossip) are circulated in this manner. When they find fertile ground (someone willing to hear and believe), the "seed" is planted and a particular way of thinking begins to take root and grow.

Example:

A friend tells you that you should have no dealings with the person you have just met. The reason your friend tells you this is that he/she does not like the person. This friend goes on to say, *"He thinks he's 'all that' because he wears nice clothes and drives a nice car! And what's more, he hardly ever speaks to anyone!"* Now your conversations with the person may have been the exact opposite. This person may have been very warm and pleasant while talking with you. Yet most of us will begin to think and act differently toward this new acquaintance because of the words or "seed" planted in our minds by our friend. Often, we will believe the rumor or negative report about a person without doing our own research. Your friend could be dead wrong! Yet if you choose to believe this rumor or opinion, you may lose out on having a new friend and (perhaps) a valuable relationship!

Television, radio, cell phones, Internet, e-mail, social networks, videos/streaming, trending, books, magazines and movies are ways in which words, thoughts and ways of thinking are distributed.

The problem here is that destructive thoughts are being *mixed* in with what is positive or good. The *weeds* are growing up alongside of the wheat!

Many times something is promoted as good or positive yet it is laced with sex, violence, cursing, drugs, etc.!

For example:

Open your eyes…Face the truth!

A rapper saying, *"I try to be positive (ya know). I keep it real! I'm trying to show those* (young people) *coming up under me that you don't have to be buck wild."* might be sending mixed messages. This person's music might be saturated with the wrongdoings that he/she has done (whether fantasy or reality) the many women or men he/she has slept with, drunkenness or how he/she had to kill somebody. (We can liken this to a porn star making a commercial, promoting sexual abstinence!)

Presently, pollutants are in almost everything seen, written or listened to.

So this is what happens. Let's imagine this same rapper has given money to buy one hundred needy children clothes and shoes. This is good and positive—helping the youth! Now let's imagine that this rapper's latest album goes platinum (one-million-plus sales)—and in his/her or videos, he/she is *"pimp smackin' hoes,"* smoking a pound of herb (marijuana), having sex with this and that girl (or guy); the lyrics reflecting what is being shown in the video.

What is so positive about this rapper?

This person has helped a little—one hundred people. But how many woman beaters, (wannabe) pimps, players, teen mothers, drug addicts, thugs—and *"hoes"* is this rapper's music (words) giving birth to? (But "It's cool though!" Hey, this person has helped one hundred people at the expense of over nine hundred thousand others.

Commercial: *This author grew up in the hip-hop culture. Moreover, much of this author's personal style and influences are derived directly from Hip Hop! Yet I've now had my eyes opened to the truth (that all words carry the power of influence). Words plant seeds that, if believed, will shape a person's thinking and their lives. I can't look at or listen to certain things anymore. (Although I struggle with this, I refuse to be entangled or return to a destructive lifestyle and way of thinking.)*

This author is in no way placing blame for the world's moral decline solely on Hip Hop. The exact same negative influences polluted nearly <u>all</u> other forms of media including: social networks, TV/movies, books—and music (Rock, Soul/

Neo Soul, Pop, R & B, Acid Rock, Jazz and Country, etc.). They are merely different ways that thoughts (words) are distributed!

Alcohol and cigarette companies (as well as others) are doing the same thing I have just explained in the example of the rapper. They market their product in such a way that they convince millions that their product will make us cooler—or that we'll get the gorgeous girl or the guy of our dreams! By buying and using their product, one will become more rugged, sexier or desirable—but in reality . . . *Not!*

Companies (with negative reputations) are currently running more and more advertisements—boasting of their charitable contributions and good deeds they are doing in various communities. Yet, the same companies continue to sell products that have and are presently killing millions of people every year. They have made billions of dollars by ensnaring and then killing their consumers. Now in a more responsible move, they are currently running ads against the use of their own products! This is done for two reasons—one is to deceive the public into thinking that such companies *"aren't so bad"*—look at how they are helping people—and two, because *any press is good press*, any publicity is good publicity!

Advertisement/marketing is a subtle word for *'brainwashing'* (or rather hypnosis or *'programming'*); the power of suggestion.

Money over morals! (This is the current way of thinking for most of us.)

- *"As long as I get mines, it's whatever."*
- Somebody dies. *"Oh well..."* Someone gets sick or hurt. *"Sorry to hear that..."*

'Brainwashing' (suggestive programming) and our Thoughts

This author will be using the word 'brainwashing' as a loose term—as well as its stronger meaning. With that being said, brainwashing (the power of suggestion) is easy. It's done all of the time. It's simply influencing someone think the way we want him/her to.

Open your eyes…Face the truth!

- Telling a "half-truth" or half the story
- Repetition—repeating something over and over again, (remember song choruses?)
- Appealing to senses and desires (hunger, thirst, lust)
    - Through seduction/enticement
    - Through bribery
    - Through promises of reward or gain

We've all been victims of brainwashing—or suggestion (marketing/advertising)!
That's why we:

- Must have the latest smart phone or tablet
- follow fads or trends—no matter how stupid
- Answer to weird nicknames: *Boo, Stink-Stink, Pooda Man,* etc. (some people don't like their nicknames—but still answer when called by it.)
- Curse use profanity (people around us are speaking it)
- Have casual sex, sleeping around
- Abuse each other (mentally and, for some of us, physically)
- Engage in drugs and alcohol usage
- Experiment with alternative lifestyles (homosexuality, lesbianism)
- Violence

We now see these things as *normal* because we have been bombarded by these abnormalities (in some way or other) over a long period of time. The first exposure was the initial '*seed*'. That *seed* was watered (through repetition and time) and now many of these abnormal ways of thinking have become "dense forests" in our minds. It may take years to cut it all down and be completely cleared away! What was once rejected /dispelled is now the norm and commonplace—even embraced. (*Remember when you couldn't say certain words on TV or radio?* It wasn't that long ago.)

Some of us like—even love, our habits and addictions! (Therefore, we continue in them.)

Some of us don't want to change!

Destructive thoughts lead to self-destruction through: (depression, sadness, anger, bitterness, promiscuity, suicide, murder)!

How can we change?

1. We must be shown that the way we are accustomed to following is incorrect and that we do not have to accept this way any longer.
2. We must receive (embrace) help in order to come up out of the incorrect thinking.
3. We must be given a standard of correct thinking that we can see for ourselves.
4. We must accept the new way of thinking and abandon the old way altogether. (Old habits die hard! It will take time.)
5. We need someone to walk with us; to teach, counsel and encourage us as we learn the new way of thinking.
6. We must practice, practice, practice the new way of thinking!

As time passes, certain ways and habits begin to fall off. Eventually, we are set free (from addictions, habits, etc.)! Once we have obtained our freedom, we must be sure not to pick them up again.

There are certain people, places and things we can no longer hang around! And there are certain things we cannot watch or listen to—or we'll become trapped again!

Remember this:

Watch what you say! Be mindful of what you watch and what you listen to!

Death and life are in the power of the tongue, and those who love it will eat its fruit. (Proverbs 18:21)

Likewise, the tongue is a small part of the body; but it makes great boasts. Consider what a great forest is set on fire by a small spark. The tongue also is a fire, a world of evil among the parts of the body. It corrupts the whole body, sets the whole course of one's life on fire, and is itself set on fire by hell. All kinds of animals, birds, reptiles, and sea creatures are being tamed and have been tamed by mankind, but no human being can tame the tongue. It is a restless evil, full of deadly poison. (James 3-6)

Out of the same mouth come praises and cursing. My brothers and sisters, this should not be. (James 3:10)

I. L. Jackson

Gloria's Story

I know this girl by the name of Gloria—a beautiful girl, who met a certain boy at the store. It was his summer job. We'll call the boy "Rob"—and (needless to say) Gloria liked him a lot! They saw each other night and day; things seemed "right as rain". Such joy! But it soon turned to pain... (I'll explain).

Rob was frustrated... we all know what he's thinking of. Rob said, *"Gloria—why can't we make love?"*

But every time Rob would ask, Gloria flatly refused! Until one day, Rob said, *"Yo... I'm confused!"* He said *"We both love each other—there is no one else... So I can't understand why you won't give yourself to me! I'm going away to school in three... You're my heart (Boo). I Love you... But this is killing me!"*

Gloria frowned and lay down, to give Rob what was sacred. She asked Rob to "be gentle..." but he was too eager to take it! He was rough! Her first time, he treated her like a "Ho"! Gloria screamed, "Please... stop!" but Rob just kept on going!

When it was over, Rob threw on his clothes and told her, *"Yo! I gotta go... I'm out... Nice to know ya!"* Poor Gloria rolled over... confused and in pain, she has become a statistic...another victim of *'the game'*. Now what was pure is now stained, overwhelmed by the shame, *"You got played..!"* echoes repeatedly through Gloria's brain!

Now to this day, it's plain to see, that Gloria's changed. She tries to *'front'* and hide the hurt—but it's too hard to maintain. She'll never be the same! Eyes filled with tears she can't restrain. Her heart's been broken...Gloria vows, *"I will NEVER love—again."*

Written by: I. L. Jackson

Open your eyes…Face the truth!

Sex/Abuse

Sex
(Sex/Abuse/Lust)

What is sex?

Sex is the name of the act by which we (humans, animals, etc.) reproduce, and it is the term we use to describe gender (*What sex is this baby? Is it a boy or is it a girl?*).

Did you know that humans (man) are the only creation that has sexual intercourse face-to-face (uh . . . humans and sea horses, I think)? Can you name any other animal that can gaze into each other's eyes while having sex?

Sex was meant to be an expression of intimate love (a man and his wife) and for reproduction.

Sex is supposed to be special; private (between a man and his wife).

Sex was not meant to be an extracurricular activity (like a sport), when one jumps from partner to partner.

Sex is/was meant for marriage.

Marriage is a commitment between two people who have decided to spend their lives together and to raise a family. When sex is misused, we can expect problems.

Having sexual desire is not wrong, it is natural!
Yet sex—because it is addictive (and can be quite dangerous because of sexually transmitted diseases)—it should not be indulged in until marriage and shared with one partner.

Sex and Multiple Partners

When we have sex, there is a connection formed with our partner that goes deeper than the physical. There is a mixing or blending together of the man and the woman spiritually. This is a permanent connection. (We call this "soul ties"). If one has had sex with numerous partners, he/she is spiritually tied to each of them and now shares some of their traits. An individual might be tied to the following: nice guys, knuckleheads; whores and or "chicken heads"; clowns, the mentally disturbed, depressed, diseased, and demonic individuals. *Woe!*

The physical manifestation of this bonding or blending of spirits is a baby.

Babies are the combination of both Daddy and Mommy; their good and their bad qualities.

It is up to the parents to protect, nurture, teach and guide their children in the way that is good and positive. If one parent is absent or slack, the child will suffer loss.

It is the job of *both* parents to cultivate the child so that that child can maximize his/her potential!

A single parent can raise a child but cannot instill within that child all that he/she needs to be well rounded.

There are some behavior traits that only the father can deal with or bring out because they are of him. There are some things that only the mother can fully understand or bring out because they are of her!

When one parent is missing or not functioning in the manner that he/she should, the family unit malfunctions and the child's development is hindered in one way or another. The child may be forced to try coping with this trait, this way of thinking, this undeveloped portion of himself or herself without that parent's help. If the one parent cannot pick up the slack in place of the missing parent, the child may begin to seek someone or something else to fill the void.

A promiscuous (whorish) girl is quite often looking for the love of her father. We've discussed this in a previous chapter. Hoping to find the love that she longs for, she may seek it through relationships with boys and men, as she gets older. What if this girl has been sexually abused and has no idea of what a father's love truly is. She might continue her search and may find only those who wish to take advantage of her.

The thug, for the most part, is searching for the wisdom, guidance and acceptance that he never received from his dad.

Dad might have been in the house yet may have never taken the time to interact with his son. Perhaps dad worked long, hard hours. It could be that he had an addiction. Perhaps Dad and Mom are separated and or divorced. Whatever the case, without a strong father figure in his life, a son may be seduced by the streets where drug dealers and gang members become his father and his family! (Many of our sons hate their fathers because "Dad walked out on Mom and me, so F@$#% him!")

Hate is actually the feeling of love that has become jealous, has been hurt or feels rejection.

We might love someone very much but if that person hurt us, if we feel hate toward that person, our hate would be as strong as our love once was. In truth, we still love that person but we've been hurt and we want them to feel what we feel.

- Alcoholism/drug addiction
- Sexual immorality
- Depression
- Suicide
- Crime

*(All of these have roots in some sort of family disorder.)

Stepparents, boyfriends or girlfriends are rarely equipped to bring out of a child the character or integrity that might lay deep within him/her because they were not meant to raise someone else's offspring.

Concerning "family unity" and family structure; *Confusion is the result when the purpose for sex is not kept.*

...And (while I'm thinking about it)

Open your eyes…Face the truth!

Divorce scars children! (Don't deceive yourself.)

Often, children are made to do the following:

- Choose one parent over the other
- Become the sounding board for the ill feelings that their parents may have for one another
- Adjust or accept
  o A missing parent
  o Substitutes (various boyfriends/girlfriends)
  o Stepmother/father

(A child's world undergoes a major upheaval. The child, in most cases, has no choice but to accept the mannerisms, ways and attitudes of this new person or people in their lives.)

- Siblings (from blending families)—brothers and sisters with a different mother or father as well as last names
- Different and or special treatment given to other siblings

This new parent (and whomever he/she brings with him or her) may be a destructive force to the child and the family as a whole. The new person may be abusive or neglectful toward the needs of the child, focusing all of his/her attention toward his/her partner.

Example: A brother or sister might receive a gift or be taken out somewhere. The other sibling(s) might not receive at all because the step-parent may say, "That's not my child!"

This is favoritism. This is rejection. It is painful. It is a deep wound to the child who has been passed over! The results are as follows:

- Low self-esteem
- Anger/bitterness
- Rejected feelings
- Depression
- Sex, drugs/alcohol experimentation and addictions

162

- Suicide
- Violence and *murder!*

Sexual Addiction/Perversion

Sexual addiction is most difficult to overcome.

This is because sexual addiction:

- Stems from natural desire. We all have sexual desire yet this does not give us an excuse to act outside of sex's proper function.
  - It is a physical expression of (spiritual) love and spiritual bonding between a man and his wife (woman)
  - It is meant for reproduction.

- Is <u>not</u> viewed as a serious problem until:

  - one catches as an STI (sexually transmitted infection)
  - one gets caught in adultery or cheating
  - one commits rape
  - one molests children
  - it becomes perverse

The mind-set that this current generation lives by: *"If it feels good—do it!"*

Unless having sex is unbearably painful (for you)—we love sex!

This is a major problem because sex is very enjoyable!

We love:

- To think about it
- To talk about it
- To watch it
- To engage in it

Open your eyes…Face the truth!

In order to conquer sexual addiction, one must admit he/she has a problem and then must desire to be set free. (Many people don't believe they have a problem.)

No one wants to stop having sex!

Even those with sexually transmitted diseases such as HIV infection still have this strong desire. Most infected persons do not stop having sex whether they are aware of their condition or not. That is why many STI's continue to spread in many areas of the world (even right here in "the good ol' United States of America").

Why is sexual addiction so strong?

Because sexual addiction is unlike other addictions—that are of the mind alone (even eating disorders have their roots in mental disorders).

Depression, low self-image, etc., have a mental cause.

Sexual addiction is both mental and physical!

Similar to the relentless and intense nagging one feels from one's stomach when one goes a long time without eating, the body craves sexual satisfaction! One's body screams, *"I need it! I must have it!"* One's mind (eventually) responds by saying, *"OK…but with whom? What? Where? When? And How?"* The body then says, *"I don't care! Just find a way!"* When the body's relentless attack or nagging becomes unbearable, the mind will find a way! This is why experimentation with drugs and alcohol is so dangerous! With drugs hindering the mind's ability to make sound decisions, the body's sexual appetite becomes a loosed animal! An individual opens him/her 'self' up to sexual perversion.

Sexual perversion occurs when the body's desires (or experiences) so overpower the mind, that all restraint is soon cast away; the individual is led away by the body's desires.

Furthermore, unlike other addictions, one can be sexually addicted without:

- feeling depressed
- feeling stressed out
- Being molested or raped
- Having low self-esteem
- Having a mental or psychological disorder

Sexual addiction **(for the most part) is the "flesh" getting its desires fulfilled (despite what the mind thinks or wants)!**

The flesh overpowers the mind!

Here we find who or what (really) controls us. For most of us, it is the flesh that runs the show! It is through sex that our flesh exerts its total authority over us! It is here that we begin to realize that everything we do and think is for *"self,"* him/her 'self' (coincidentally "self" spelled backward is "fles"—add an "h" for his or her and you have "flesh").

- We seek money:
    o So that our *flesh* can have pleasure
    o So that we can put fancy things on our *flesh*
- We buy cars so as not to tire out the *flesh* by walking
- We invented the microwave oven and fast food so that our *flesh* can have time to pursue other interests, etc., etc.

Think about it: We invent things so that our *'flesh'* won't have to work so hard.

Someone might say, *"Well, not everyone is or will become sexually addicted."*

This is true. There are some who:

- have (over time) found deliverance through abstinence (but should they ever indulge again . . .)
- are virgins (as long as they do not have sex they will not be plagued with this addiction, although they may feel pressured and be tempted)
- have been molested, abused or raped and have shut down sexually

Open your eyes…Face the truth!

If one has ever had sex, one's body has experienced its greatest pleasure! (It will continue to crave it again and again!) One who has had sex cannot say, *"I'm not addicted!"* because sex's influence saturates every aspect of our lives! Thus bombarding us, feeding our minds with sexual thoughts that will eventually influence us to act out!

Look around! Sex is everywhere (TV, radio, posters, billboards, books, magazines, video games, social media etc., etc.)!

There is no escaping sex's influence. Unless one was to move to the mountains and become a hermit, but even then one would see the animals doing their thing!

Sex affects the poor and the powerful, the educated and the ignorant, kings, princes—and presidents, the employed and the unemployed alike!

Note: Masturbation is a sign of sexual addiction! We may think we are not addicted but when we engage in masturbation, we *are* giving in to our body's demand for gratification. We are giving control of ourselves to our bodies.

If one were to watch, hear or engage in something sexually hot, how would one react? Would a burning fire be ignited, begging to rage even hotter? How long could one resist one's own body? Would it cause a reaction (two, three, four days later, maybe a week, a month or so)? One's flesh will torment one's mind! Some are strong enough to resist and suppress their fleshly desires. Others may find something to occupy themselves so as not to indulge—but the memories will flood one's mind with graphic images of sensual pleasure!

At the most inopportune moments, those nasty thoughts harass and distract us!

Know this! If one habitually masturbates, that person can say, *"It is true. I am addicted…"* (Queue the dramatic music… *dun, dun, dunnn…!*)

Abuse, Rape and Sex

Sex was meant to be an act shared by consenting married adults!

Sex was not meant to (or should ever) be forced upon a person!
Women who have been raped (for the most part):

- Feel violated (like some vital part of them has been stolen)
- Feel dirty inside (unclean)
- Feel fear, anger, hatred
- Feel helplessness
- May be traumatized for years (life)

Something happens mentally.

- Some shut down
- Some don't want to be touched (by husbands, by their sons, by men, in general)

It's rape! Violent, horrible, forceful, merciless!

Many victims develop a warped view of sex!

Some women:

- Equate sex with rape, seeing both as the same
- Turn to lesbianism (having sex with other women), not wanting to be touched by brutish men
- Develop a distrust and hatred toward all men

Children and Sexual Abuse

It is truly heartbreaking to hear that a child has been raped or molested!

Children feel they have no choice.

- They are threatened ("I'll do this or that," "I'll hurt Mommy," or—"I'll hurt you").
- They are told it's a game ("Keep it a secret.").

- They are bribed with money or candy to keep and told not to say anything.
- They may love their abuser; and therefore not want any negative consequences to happen to him/her.

Some children are be beaten, yelled at, ignored, threatened and told they are liars when they have told.

Countless children have grown up—are now adults with children—and have never told anyone that they have been raped or molested.

How many of us have grown up with a warped perception of sex and love?

A Young Boy (Molested by a Female)

- May actually like the experience and desire that it continues
- Creates lust, excessive and aggressive sexual desire
- May harass female classmates
- May become a "Peeping Tom"
- Sows seeds for pornographic addiction (movies, magazines, Internet) and masturbation
- Sees and treats all women as sex objects
- Feels that expressing love means to have sex *("If we are not having sex, you are not showing me love. You do not love me.")*
- The line between friend and "love interest" may be blurred or non-existent (resulting in offense, hurt feelings and broken relationships)
- Multiple sexual encounters (more than one baby's mama)
- May becomes a rapist or molester himself (pedophile)
- May enjoy being touched or groped by females; desiring it always

A Young Boy (Male Molester)

- Has low self-esteem, may become reclusive
- Feels abnormal, feels as if he doesn't fit in

- May become overly macho in order to hide or cover shame or homosexual thoughts and memories
- Definite warped perception of sex
- May turn to homosexuality (may openly display feminine characteristics, may cross-dress and/or desire to have a sex change)
- May become violent, angry and bitter (because of perverse sexual thoughts and feelings of being violated)
- May not want to be touched in any way (will violently defend a certain space around himself)
- May turn to drugs/alcohol as a means to drown, block memories or simply cope with the experience as well as the feelings that came with it.

As I've said it before, sex is enjoyable and addictive!

Some (individuals) have been raped or molested and find that they enjoy and prefer to have sex in that manner. (I speak of men and women, boys and girls).

Having sex is like doing drugs!

Once again, there are some victims who have (secretly) enjoyed the experience of being raped or molested. This author has spoken to a few victims who shared the following:

- Feelings/believing that having sex is the way to show love or to make others love us
- Insatiable desire to have sex resulting in frequent masturbation and promiscuity (having numerous sexual encounters)
- Prostitution, porn star—using sex as a way to make money or obtain the things one desires
- Inordinate relationships (homosexuality, lesbianism, bisexuality—orgies)

Commercial:

This author has come in contact with some individuals that have been raped or molested repeatedly (from several months to several years). As a result, these individuals have learned to somehow "disconnect" themselves (their minds) from their bodies. They mentally leave the room—yet their bodies remain! If such a person were to grow up and get married, never having dealt with the horrifying experiences of his/her past, he/she will continue this behavior during sex with his/her spouse. There are going to be problems! One spouse is doing all he/she can to express his/her love while the other spouse lays there like a corpse. Literally, there is only one person in the room!

Pornography

Pornography is anything that uses sex as a means of entertainment and to stimulate us sexually. (This includes magazines, phone lines, videos, playing cards, books, certain web sites, etc.)

Pornography causes awakens/feeds 'lust'.

Lust is extreme or excessive desire.

- o Lust manifests through:
  - Heightened sex drive
  - Masturbation (satisfying one's sexual desire by one's self)
  - Experimentation in youth and small children (incest)
  - Harassment, humping, grinding, swirling and rape (force)
  - Teen pregnancies
  - Child molesting
  - Promiscuity (having sexual encounter after sexual encounter)
  - Disinterest in one's husband or wife (disconnection, withdrawal of affection)

Here, we are forced to face the truth—and that is, *'lust'* is the force behind sexual addiction. *Lust* is trapped in our flesh and it is the *"strong man"* that pushes us into compromising situations. Lust is _never_ ever satisfied! Lust never says enough! Lust screams and hollers, begs, pleads, coaxes and persuades. Lust does whatever is necessary to get what it desires. Lust does not care if you or the other person is married, whether you are a man or woman of God; it cares nothing about rules, regulations or age limits. Lust screams, *"I must have . . . ! Gimme!* And *"Get it!"* Lust whispers, *"Just one time!"* and *"No one will ever know!"* Lust convinces us to take what is not ours. It uses our hurts, loneliness, self-esteem issues, frustrations, inadequacies, fears, etc. Lust hides within those things waiting for the opportunity to have its desires met. Lust is an opportunist and sees every situation as a chance to have its way! Lust overrides the will of the mind, our judgment and our ability to reason.

This is how the world's system operates! It caters to our lust, bombarding us with things that increase our selfish desires—*"...lust of the flesh lust of the eyes and pride in possessions"*. We become cold and uncaring toward others and their needs as well as blinded to our own ignorance, insensitivity and weaknesses. We become so caught up in appeasing our lusts we don't even notice certain rights and freedoms being stripped away from us. We hurt ourselves and others as we race to fulfill our various lusts.

Lust has no morals, no code of conduct and no regrets! I am not just talking about sex here! Lust also desires riches, fame, houses, cars, respect, power—and anything else that will make our *flesh* happy! Lust gets what it wants and once it controls our hearts, it controls the whole person (self-destruction is not far away)! *"How can this be?"* or *"How is this done?"* you *might ask.*

Pornography is the start of a cycle!

The ages in which we are exposed to pornography are increasingly younger and younger. We use sex to sell cars, beer, CDs and DVDs, videos, movies (even PG and PG13), songs, magazines, books, etc. "Smart phones" with internet access, social networks, face time, text messaging/sexting are a part of today's culture. It is easy to become exposed to pornography. This is how it starts and is maintained; distracting us from work, school and anything productive.

Pornography sows seeds that are remembered and eventually carried out!

- Males see females as sex objects:

- o Not having (or caring if they have) their own opinions, minds or intelligence
- o Not having ideas, dreams or goals
- o Not having emotions, not caring for their feelings

- Females see themselves:
  - o As having power to get what they want, to manipulate and to control
  - o Using sex as a means to receive love from a boy/man ("If I don't give him some, he won't like me.")
  - o Using sex to be liked or to become popular
  - o Using sex to *"get what I want"* This can lead to prostitution (selling sex):

    - For money
    - To get hair and nails done
    - To get clothes
    - To pay rent and bills
    - To buy furniture
    - To buy food

Teens and Sex

Having sex can lead to the following:

- Breakups and being deeply hurt
- Numerous sexual encounters
- Cheating and getting dumped
- Physical and mental abuse (someone becoming obsessed or possessive)

Girls

- Pregnancy

  - More than one baby's daddy
  - Little/no help (from daddy) raising child(ren)

- Used for sex (hit and run)
- Hindered goals
- Stress, depression, anger, hopelessness
- Financial struggle

Baggage! Baggage! Baggage!

A young girl with a baby is a target for boys wanting sex. They can see she's done it at least once before!

Boys

- Multiple children by more than one mother

    o Child support garnished wages (possible arrears)
    o Hindered and unfulfilled dreams and goals
    o Financial struggle
    o Jail (for statutory rape; failing to pay child support)
    o Hustling (selling drugs) or "under the table" jobs, needing more than one job)
    o Unwanted stress

Also

- Sexually transmitted diseases (STI's)
    o Gonorrhea
    o Chlamydia
    o Crabs (genital lice)
    o Herpes, Syphilis, Genital warts and HIV/AIDS (all of which have no known cure)

This author encourages you to wait for marriage! (I know. People are going to do what they want to do regardless of the danger.)

Wait! And again I say… Wait!

Below is a list of the unfair expectations we put on our spouses (going into marriage) because of our previous sexual experiences:

- He or she just doesn't make me feel it like (some other person once did).
- He or she's boring.
- This person reminds me of... but it just isn't the same
- If only his or her body was like (some person from our past).
- I'm used to having sex daily but he or she has a low sex drive...
- "Hold up . . . ! He or she has changed!"
- My former lover was . . .
  - More romantic
  - Bigger
  - freakier/wilder
  - muscular/shapely
  - tender/affectionate
  - loving
  - rich, wealthy
  - more handsome/prettier
  - more rugged or macho, lady like, etc.

Sadly, if our spouse fails to meet up with our expectations, most of us will make him or her pay for their shortcomings.

Most people will:

- Withdraw from them
- Give them the silent treatment
- Display anger/resentment toward them
- Show coldness and irritation when our spouses are around
- Argue and pick fights
- Bash, insult and/or degrade our spouses
- Find fault with everything our spouses do
- Never be satisfied with our spouse's efforts (no matter what he/she has done or is doing)
- Be critical of everything concerning our spouse's height, weight, shape, clothes, mannerisms, etc.
- Neglect our spouses emotionally and sexually
- Be merciless toward any shortcomings or mistakes our spouses make

We tend to treat our spouses unfairly because they are not fulfilling an experience that we are secretly trying to recapture—through them.

The results may be as follows:

- Spouse may shut down
- Cheating (the spouse might seek positive affirmation from someone else and have an affair)
- Fighting/abuse
- Separation/divorce
- Bitterness/resentment
- Hatred (our spouse may grow to hate us for our ill treatment toward them)
- Murder (in extreme cases)

Sex is a weapon!

- Used to manipulate
    - o As a reward for giving or buying (me) food, clothes, furniture, getting my nails and hair done, etc.
    - o Withheld if one has been displeased or disappointed (to get one's way).
    - o It is used in politics, espionage and warfare to distract (taking the focus off of the things that should be focused upon) and to get the enemy to slack defensively. It is also used to infiltrate, to gain information and to destroy (one's reputation) through scandal and shame!

To some degree, sex is used as a weapon of mass destruction!

- To so engross us, that we become unproductive
- To saturate us with disease and (through drugs/alcohol addiction) to cripple the next generation with physical and psychological deficiencies
- To promote a "babies having babies" ideology so that mind-sets can be shaped without resistance (train a child to do anything while he is still

young and when he/she is old, he/she shall continue to practice it out of habit!)

"Babies" *are* having babies. Parents, who are little more than babies themselves, will train their children in their ways. The result is a generation whose ways are childish and more rebellious, selfish, prideful, disrespectful; having less restraint than the first! This is because most babies that have babies:

- Despise correction or being told what to do, so they raise their children in the same manner (they will not let others correct their children). They do not discipline their children (when the child is doing wrong). Rather, immature parents tend to correct their children only when their children are getting on *their* nerves (i.e. interfering with some activity or pleasure that interests that parent)!
- Do not teach their children manners and other social skills because they lack such knowledge themselves
- Treat their babies like new toys. Once the baby becomes older, the parent seems to lose interest, seeking to party and recapturing their own lives.
- Drag their children to places and into adult situations that they should not be exposed to (Rated-R movies, arguments, adult conversations, abusive situations, etc.).
- Openly show resentment and hostility toward the child for being a hindrance to their lives or toward their mate, who is not acting or doing what he/she should be doing (example, a deadbeat dad or unreasonable mother).

How is sex used for mass destruction?

Eventually, our leaders will resign or die off. Who will replace them? Those who are of the following generation(s)! The coming generations are more wicked, less educated, brutish, ruthless, and replete with mental/emotional issues; not to mention being lazy and sluggish! Those who are educated, productive and peaceable are decreasing in number!

What will be the result if this remnant were to be removed?

Without a strong, educated generation to follow this one, lawlessness will result! Media will be able to control the majority of the masses through their "programming" (broadcasts). Do you remember a show called Max headroom? Because people will have no restraint, justice will easily be snatched. There will be a lack of sane leadership, no true government that is for, of and by the people. Those who have power would enslave and oppress those who have wallowed in ignorance and have found it to be bliss. Those ignorant souls will never see the trap until it has snapped shut and they find all of their rights and privileges taken away! They will say, *"While we were drunk, acting wild, having orgies, and indulging ourselves, they were stealing our freedom! How did we become so blind?"* (This is not some fantasy. This is the truth! Look around!)

What's the message? Is it true? Is it good for me and you?

Flee from sexual immorality. All other sins a person commits are outside the body, but whoever sins sexually, sins against their own body. (1 Corinthians 6:18)

Do you not know that he who unites himself with a prostitute is one with her in body? For it is said, The two will be one flesh." (1 Corinthians 6:16)

Marriage should be honored by all, and the marriage bed kept pure, for God will judge the adulterer and all the sexually immoral. (Hebrews 13:4)

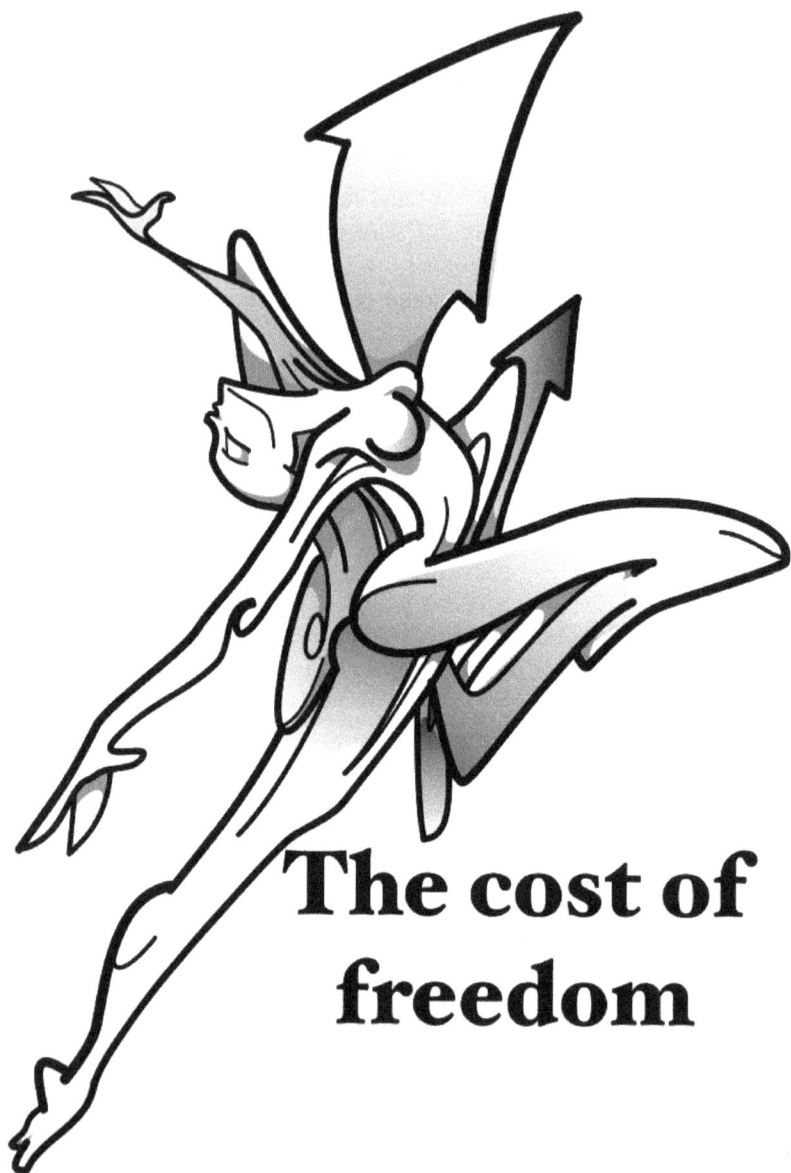

The cost of freedom

The cost of freedom

What is freedom?

Freedom is the state, which affords one the privilege or right to make choices, not being under the control of anyone or anything.

What is mental freedom?

It is a mind that is not under the control of certain ways of thinking.

- Positive mental freedom. This is a mind freed from negative or destructive thinking (addictions/strongholds). This is the mind of someone who can find the good in all things, has high self-esteem and is optimistic even when things are going against them.
- Negative mental freedom. This is *false* freedom, one whose mind has no restraints or fears! (This is the mind of the foolish.) The person with this mind may not have low self-esteem (per se) but rather has a "me against the world" or "the world is mine" attitude. This is the mentality of many who are rich: *"It's all about me," "I'm out to get mines!"* and *"I can buy or make my own rules!"* Although this person's self-esteem may be high, there is an arrogance there that may prove to be this person's downfall!

Both are possibility thinkers, yet the individual that has false freedom lacks one essential element. False freedom is tainted because of selfishness—and therefore lacks love. That selfishness, which is rooted in pride, will cause the person with false freedom to fall! On this individual's way to the top, many others may be stepped on, used, and cut off. The loss of friendships, family, and other relationships truly confirm the statement. *"It's lonely at the top!"* And yet another statement applies here. *"What goes up must come down!"* The person that is falsely freed may soon find that he/she lacks fulfillment because there is no one (true friends) there to share his/her success. In fact, this person will become jealous when the spotlight shifts from him/her to someone else. Again, this is *not* true freedom. This person is (actually) enslaved by pride, which creates selfishness on the way up, jealousy and suspicion on the way down—and in the end, self-destruction!

One can never truly appreciate freedom unless one has experienced the shame and bondage of being enslaved.

The opposite of freedom is slavery.

A slave is one who is under the complete control of someone or something else (we have discussed this before). Every aspect of a slave's life is controlled by the will of another person or thing.

One can be enslaved to a person or group of persons. A group of people can be enslaved by another group of people. One can also be enslaved to a substance or way of thinking.

One can be enslaved to:

- Drugs/alcohol. Substance abuse stems from destructive thinking. The addiction may have been acquired while seeking relief from loneliness, frustration, pain, and grief; or a person was influenced by continued exposure (TV or radio, family, etc.), was pressured into by peers (desiring to be accepted, looking or being seen as cool), or was passed down through the family's lineage (disorders and diseases).
- Destructive ways of thinking. Violence, fighting, theft, and other illegal acts. Destructive ways of thinking also includes mistreatment of or the abuse of one's own body (numerous sex partners, unprotected sex, body piercing and numerous tattoos) and how one interacts with others. A person who has no regard or respect for others' feelings, property, or safety, not even one's own well-being is a self-destructive

thinker. This person does not judge correctly and has no wisdom or understanding. Their decisions cause more and more trouble!

These oppressors (drugs and destructive thought patterns) are the enemies to freedom and freethinking because one is literally trapped, bound, and made to do the will of his/her master.

We are enslaved to whomever or whatever we serve with our bodies (whether person or thing)!

Who or what are you enslaved to?

- Sex. Pornography, masturbation, frequent sexual encounters with different partners. One may find most of one's thoughts and time are spent attempting to satisfy one's sexual appetite; venturing into the perverse
- Drugs. Cigarettes, alcohol, cocaine, crack, heroin, ecstasy (X), marijuana. One may find that one cannot stop using even though one's health and lifestyle may be suffering!
- TV/Music/Video games. These things may occupy most of one's time to the point that one is unable to accomplish anything else (nor does one desire to do anything). Productivity and imagination suffers here!
- Friends (as well as boyfriend/girlfriend). They may tell you where to go. What to do, how long to be there, etc.
- Poverty. It controls what you can and cannot do! Poverty controls what one will or will not eat, how one dresses, where one lives, and where one can go!

Do you wish to remain a slave?

Each one of us must make a decision to remain a slave or to break free.

Destructive thinking leads to misery, broken relationships, sickness, perhaps prison, and (eventually) death!

Free thinking leads to wisdom, strong relationships, and longer life (comparably).

The price of freedom is costly but worth everything you will go through to gain it!

In order to achieve freedom, something must die! (Our old way of thinking must be put to death!)

Changing one's way of thinking from *negative* to *positive* is painful, requiring much work and time. Denying one's self of the thing(s) one has been enslaved to is an uncomfortable, time-consuming struggle with self. This is called *mortifying one's flesh or dying to self* (this cannot be done without assistance). It can be a long tedious process, but it's worth it! No pain, no gain!

Freedom is not gained without some loss happening (first): loss of position, status, job, friends, etc. It requires going beyond what was once familiar and comfortable to us. We must leave our comfort zone and venture out into unexplored territory.

The old way of thinking must be unlearned (discarded, kicked to the curb) at the same time a new way must be introduced and taught, thus replacing the negative with that which is positive. Ignorance is replaced with knowledge!

Darkness is replaced with light!

The old way of thinking or "the way we always did it" seems more comfortable than the new. Yet we must be determined not to return to the old way because that path led us into a world of troubles (although it might have been fun for a time)!

Don't be like everyone else. Break out! *Get free!*

Many have lost their lives to gain or to maintain their freedom. One example of dying for the cause of freedom is that of the many soldiers who have died (worldwide) in defense of their countries!

I have mentioned Ms. Harriet Tubman before regarding freedom—how she struggled and obtained her own, then how she returned to help many others to gain theirs. Let's look (again) at why she (and others throughout history who have gained their freedom) was so successful.

- She was aware of her self-worth. She thought highly of herself. She considered her enslaved condition and rejected it! (Ms. Tubman wanted to be more than those who were around her, who accepted slavery as their lot in life)!
- She did not let fear stop her! She was determined!
- She did not compromise!
- She pressed on (even when others wanted to give up)!
- Once she obtained her own freedom, she used the same method to help free others!
- She couldn't take certain people! Some people had to be left behind. They would have hindered her progress, given up, been recaptured or killed, betrayed her, and caused her to be recaptured. They would have messed up everything, and everyone would have suffered!
- She used only certain paths!
  - She knew she could not go down certain ways or go to certain places, nor could she stay too long in other places. (This is extremely important.)
  - She only traveled at certain times. She understood the importance of waiting and moving when the time was right. She didn't just run out!

Being free does not mean that one can go anywhere and do whatever one pleases!

Great responsibility comes with being free. If it is not adhered to, one will easily become enslaved again or even killed!

(We've mentioned this before, but hey, some things are worth repeating.)

When a slave would escape during Harriet Tubman's time, he would be tortured and guarded all the more! Many runaways were maimed; others were killed. This was done to break the slaves' spirits. Runaways would be far less likely to try a second attempt if beaten half to death or made lame! Also, if anyone else had thoughts of breaking free, they would be too fearful of suffering the consequences were they to escape and then be recaptured. Such is the condition of those who've experienced mental freedom only to fall back or to relapse into their former condition or state. They soon find that their present condition (being recaptured) is worse than before!

Commercial: *Did you know that they (slave owners) also attempted to make slaves of Native Americans but were unsuccessful because of their fighting spirit?*

The Native Americans, being a proud and noble people, would rather fight and die than to live as slaves! I pray that we all will adopt that same spirit when it comes to freeing ourselves from mental enslavement!

(Once again I encourage you to read the "Willie Lynch Letter," which can be found on the Internet or get it in book form by Lushena Books. Lushenabks@yahoo.com.) No plug here, just sharing where I found it.

Let's return to our original thought.

Certain things cannot be done, certain paths cannot be taken, and certain people cannot come along! Our freedom will be jeopardized! We might lose everything we've worked so hard to obtain!

To stray, even a little, could mean the loss of freedom!

Freedom says, *"Yes, I can to do this or that—but I understand that some choices have negative consequences."*

Slavery says, *"I have no choice(s)."*

What are you willing to give up, that you might gain your freedom?

It could be the difference between:

- Having good health or sickness and disease
- Being successful or a failure
- Having wealth or living in poverty
- Having a fulfilled life or regrets, misery, and death

How does one get free?

- You must see yourself in your present state. (Be honest.)
- You must realize where that present state is leading you (self-destruction, jail, unemployment line, etc.)
- You must see an example of someone who is doing what you desire to do and going where you want to go. (This goes for anything you are trying to do.)
- You must make a decision. *Do you want to remain in that state?*
- You must study the habits of the one you wish to be like.
- You must then apply what you have seen and learned from that person to your own life!

You must keep going! Don't give up (or you will not obtain)! Even if you fall from time to time, get up and keep following that person's example!

You can't let anyone or anything stop or hold you back! You must succeed! You will succeed!!

Remember: Freedom isn't arrogant! It's sober in its thinking, and it is responsible in its actions!

There is one who is able to set us free and whoever He frees is *truly* free!

Wretched man that I am! Who will set me free from the body of this death? (Romans 7:24)

She will bear a Son; and you shall call his name Jesus, for He will save his people from their sins. (Matthew 1:21)

"And you will know the truth and the truth will make you free." (John 8:32)

Therefore there is no condemnation for those who are in Christ Jesus. For the law of the Spirit of life in Christ Jesus has set you free from the law of sin and of death. (Romans 8:1-2)

Appreciate the process

Appreciate the process

What is the process?

The process is the training experiences and steps one goes through to reach an expected goal.

The process is (also) the series of changes by which something grows and develops. (A caterpillar goes through a process called metamorphosis in order to become a butterfly.)

Consider this:

Before one is allowed to fight in the armed forces, one usually goes through boot camp. This means rigorous training, physical, mental, and emotional hardship. The process begins with the stripping away of all things learned (old ways and habits) so that a new, more effective way can be taught. This process involves pain, frustration, denial of personal wants (such as luxuries, etc.).Though (seemingly) long and painful, the result is a lean, mean fighting machine! A boy has been transformed into a man, and more than that, he is a soldier! This is a man or woman, who is self-controlled; capable of enduring in any climate/weather, hostile terrain, and situations; and able to think clearly and to respond with decisiveness and force if need be! This is a person with courage, honor, reliability, and strength. He/she is an asset to friends, family, and country (and all of this because he or she has gone through a process)!

Open your eyes…Face the truth!

How does one bake a cake?

To bake a cake, one needs the necessary ingredients: eggs, flour, baking soda, sugar, butter, milk, and special or secret ingredients. Yet just having all of these (ingredients) gathered in one place does not produce a cake. The ingredients must be measured, mixed together, poured into a prepared cake pan, placed into an oven (preset to the precise temperature), and allowed to bake for a certain amount of time. If one desires to have baking success, one must follow these steps! This too is an example of the process!

How does one learn to read or write? Does one just pick up a novel and begin to read the words, having no prior education?

No! One is not born with the ability to read! One must learn each letter of the alphabet and the corresponding sounds it makes. Then one must learn about vowels and consonants, how letters sound when they are put together with other letters (and so on). One must also practice writing each letter over and over again. There is a process. These things take time!

We must learn to appreciate the process (in whatever we may be going through and whatever that process may be!).

The process may include learning to work with those that you do not like, under unfavorable conditions. Going through such experiences builds character. The process may be long and very painful. One will lose many of the things one once thought one needed. Yet, in the end, one may find that those same things were distractions, hindrances, and unprofitable!
Appreciate the process! No pain, no gain!

The process involves preparation, repetition, and time!

The process involves pain, sacrifice, and loneliness at times (like being a caterpillar in a cocoon). People will not always understand the process that you are going through, your mind-set, your patience, and your determination! (However, they will all be amazed when you emerge as a beautiful butterfly!)

What do you want to be? What is your dream?

How do you plan to accomplish or to attain what you want? What's your plan?

What are you willing to give up? What you willing to change or leave behind?

Reaching Your Goal

First, one should have a goal. Next, one should develop a plan. Lastly, one should be willing to follow that plan until the goal is reached!

Reaching any goal takes:

- **Faith.** It is your belief in God, and it is putting what you believe into action. This means trusting in God to guide you in your decision making and actions. (Faith starts and ends with God).
- **Courage.** It is to stand up against all opposition, to defend what you are trying to accomplish (even if no one else believes or helps).
- Consistency. The ability or practice of staying with a thing ("stick to-it" attitude).
- **Hard work.** It is putting one's heart to productiveness, constant practice, sweat and time.

"You need a strong reason for doing what you do. If your reason "why" is strong enough, it will keep you going when times get rough"—Dr. Walter Swinson.

(Without these five attributes, one will NOT reach and maintain one's goals.)

Know Yourself

Ask yourself ten times, *"Who am I?"* Write down your responses (each question should have a different answer). This will help you to get to know you!

- You must know who you are!
- What does God say about? Who does He say you are? (Don't know? Find out?)

- You must think highly of yourself! You must like who you are!
- You must know your strengths and also your weaknesses (examine yourself, be honest).
- You must be willing and determined to change negative behaviors and habits. Change does not happen overnight! (You didn't become the person you are or get into your present circumstances overnight. It took time!) Change takes time and practice!

You must press toward your goal!

If we continue to dwell on things, saying, "This is the way it is," then things will stay the same. Yet if we set our thoughts on things "as they could be," then change will begin to take place (depressing situations, current job, house, relationship circumstances, environment, music, etc.).
If we change our minds, our actions will soon follow!

The thing(s) we rehearse over and over again:

- Become more familiar!
- Become more comfortable!
- Become stronger, harder to uproot, and get rid of!
- We become better at!

(This holds true for anything positive or negative.)

Focus on the positive!

Appreciate the process!

If you are young:

- Obey your parents!
- Do your best in school! Do your homework!
- Do your chores!

If you are young at heart:

- Do your job! Submit to your boss!
- Don't dwell on what is or what was. Set your heart on what could be!
- Don't give up!
- Don't give in!
- Stay with it! Hold your ground! Press forward!

(You) SUCK! + PROGRESS= SUCCESS!

Once again, appreciate the process!

Such were some of you; but you were washed, but you were sanctified, but you were justified in the name of the Lord Jesus Christ and in the Spirit of our God. (1 Corinthians 6:11)

Like newborn babies, long for the pure milk of the word, so that by it you may grow in respect to salvation, if you have tasted the kindness of the Lord. (1 Peter2:2-3)

Sanctify them in the truth; Your word is truth. (John 17:17)

I beseech you therefore, brethren, by the mercies of God, that ye present your bodies a living sacrifice, holy, acceptable unto God, which is your reasonable service. And be not conformed to this world; but be ye transformed by the renewing of your mind, that you may prove what is that good, and acceptable, and perfect, will of God. (Romans 12:2)

Therefore, having these promises, beloved, let us cleanse ourselves from all defilement of the flesh and spirit, perfecting holiness in the fear of the Lord. (2 Corinthians 7:1)

Open your eyes...Face the truth!

The Witness

Adam sinned,
God and man's relationship ends
We were promised a coming "Savior"
But nobody knew when.
Then came *Jesus*, the Christ
Didn't act as we thought,
Hoped he'd deliver us through war
But that was not how *he* fought.
He came to "save" what was lost.
Very great was the cost!
Jesus took our sins upon *him*
And was nailed to a cross!
He died and rose again!
Now sits high above
One died to save many
That's how God showed *His* love!
We were *"hell-bound"*
Held down—slaves to *"sin"*
And we say we choose *"hell"*
...*If we reject him*—
Jesus!
God and Christ are *"one"*!
You can't get to *"the Father"*
Without going through *"the Son"*
"The Chosen One", our Lord...
He *fulfilled* God's plan...
To *mend* the separation
Between God and Man!

Written by: I. L. Jackson

Open your eyes...Face the truth!

Truth

The truth isn't debatable! It simply is!

By now, it is apparent that we all are messed up in some way (some more than others). Whether we were corrupted through things we have inherited from our parents, things learned from the media (TV, radio, Internet, movies, magazines, etc.), through drug abuse, sex, violence, racism, *"lust of the eye, lust of our flesh, or the pride of life*, the truth is we (mankind) are totally incapable of saving ourselves from ourselves! The truth is...

This generation continues to run the "course which leads to destruction" that was started by previous generations.

We are exposed to corruption in the womb. We are born (seemingly) innocent, however as we get older, (like a virus that has entered a computer damaging its programming) we act out what we were programmed to do! Many viruses (I speak of corrupt and wicked thought patterns) have infected the programming of our youth (and all of us, for that matter)! We pass these corrupt ways to our children in much the same manner as we pass physical traits, high blood pressure, crack/alcohol addiction and AIDS!

This generation is more corrupt than the generation before it and the next generation will surpass this one in its wickedness if change is not made! We (grown-ups) have taught them! We have trained them in our ways and now we marvel at their lack of respect, rebellious attitudes, lack of fear and shame, their boldness, their intelligence, their height (stature), strength and the wickedness of their hearts. We parents, aunts and uncles, big brothers and sisters, business owners, teachers, politicians--and even presidents all have contributed to our society's moral decline and the corruption of this generation! How is this? Well, we continue to allow social media, TV, radio, etc., to bombard our youth with every kind of wickedness under the sun (even fighting against and mocking those who attempt to censor what is being seen and heard. (Remember C. Deloris Tucker? How many rappers have disrespected her in their rhymes?) We continue to teach immorality through our actions. This (present) generation has surpassed the previous generations in their wickedness! This generation is doing things bigger, better, and at a younger age than what we (ourselves) have done!

If you corrupt the youth, you destroy the future! It was all planned destroy ourselves (individually) and destroy one another! This was the plan against all of mankind from the first man until now, even to the future, and the result will shock you!

What can we do then? How can we stop this vicious cycle?

We can't stop it! The corruption will continue and get worse! But we, that have the truth, can share (that truth) with our children and others who will believe and then walk in the knowledge of the truth! (The simplicity of the next statement is where we need to start!)

> *Train up a child in the way he should go, and when he is old he shall not depart from it. (Proverbs 22:6, NKJV)*

This is the key! *But what is the way that a child should go?*

Let us look at some deeper truths.

Man (the human race) is prone to do evil or to *sin*. The evidence is the steady decline of morals and the increase of corruption, sex and violence.

Sin and Iniquity

Open your eyes…Face the truth!

What is sin?

Sin is transgression; disobedience; fault; an error in judgment; rebellion against authority, against what is right and just, and moreover, against God! (Strong's Exhaustive Concordance, Listings [2398-2403] p. 38 of the Hebrew and Chaldees dictionary and listings [264-266] p. 10 Greek Dictionary of the New Testament)

Iniquity is wickedness! (Strong's Exhaustive Concordance, Listing [5771] p. 86 of the Hebrew and Chaldees dictionary and listing [93, p. 8; 458 p. 12] Greek Dictionary of the New Testament)

Every man, woman, boy and girl was born with *sin* and *iniquity (evil, wickedness)* in their hearts.

Have you ever wished harm on someone (even if it was never spoken out loud), ever steal anything, ever looked at another man's wife or a woman's husband, desiring that you could have her? Have you ever cursed anyone out or struck anyone in a violent way? Have you had casual sex? Have you ever bought something that was stolen, or have you ever lied? (Shall I keep going?)

Satan's influence is everywhere!

Who is Satan?

Satan is the name of the adversary. He is the Accuser and the Devil. Satan means to oppose, to go against, or to withstand. (Strong's Exhaustive Concordance, Old Testament listing [7854] p. 115 of the Hebrew and Chaldees dictionary and New Testament listing [4567] p. 65 of the Greek Dictionary)

Whom does Satan oppose?

He opposes God!

God's name is 'YHWH" (YAHWEH) translated (Jehovah)! He is the Father, the creator and the source of all things (Genesis 1:1). He is holy (set apart, as mentioned in Isaiah 6:3). He is pure and righteous! He is just (1 John

1:9). He is a consuming fire (Hebrew 12:29). *"In him, there is no sin"* (1 John 3:5).

(*Jehovah, Exodus 6:3 of the Holy Bible, [self-Existent, the Eternal Strong's Exhaustive Concordance listing [3068] p. 47 Hebrew and Chaldees Dictionary)

Satan's nature (his disposition, who he is) is *against* God. He *opposes* of God in every way (however, he is not equal to God)! He is evil and corrupt. He is a liar and is *"the father of lies"* (John 8:44) who bends or adds to the truth so that wrong appears right.

This is Satan's plan: His desire is to corrupt and to blind mankind—turning our hearts away from our maker. God is "existence" (i. e. life). Satan desires to replace God as God, thus discrediting all that God has made. His desire is destruction and death!

Satan tempts us, drawing us away (from God) through *lust*. Lust (we know) is intense (selfish) desire—our own desires! Some desire money, sex, and power— and they will do almost anything to get them! Satan exploits and blinds us through our selfishness so that we will never see or understand our own sinfulness—or God's love for us; therefore, most people do not turn to God so that He may save them and cleanse them from the corruption of this world.

Satan is also known as the *"prince of the power of the air"* (the internet, social media, TV and radio waves, gossip, rumors). *Get it?* (See Ephesians 2:2.)

Satan's end will be that he (and all who follow him) will be thrown into the lake of fire to burn forevermore!

Those that say, *"There is no God,"* and all those who do not follow after God (in their hearts) will be forever separated—from God. Their end is destruction in hell.

"God will ultimately let you have it your way'! If you spend your life avoiding and running away from God, He will grant your wish! God will cast you out and separate you from His power, presence and provision forever!" (Dr. Walter Swinson)

The universe was made in perfect harmony to function as one symphony of light, color, sound (music), and beings (us), all glorifying the Almighty God!

- Sin has caused disruption, discord, and disharmony.
- Sin has entered the earth, causing rumblings, earthquakes, volcanic eruptions, and so on.
- The entire planet has been corrupted through and through. This corruption has caused a ripple effect throughout the universe, which is indeed one body and is God's "body" (not His actual body, but this means he owns and runs it all).

When Adam (the first man) sinned, he *"fell"* (out of God's covering, glory and was kicked out of God's presence). Because Adam was the very first man everyone born after him (all of us) are *'fallen'*!

Because of this, just as sin entered into the world through one man, and death through sin, so also death passed to all men, because all sinned. (Romans 5:12- Berean Literal Translation.)

Fallen—*thrown down*, die, cause to perish, cease, fugitive, to be judged (Strong's Exhaustive Concordance listing [5307] p. 79, Hebrew and Chaldees Dictionary)

Eventually, sin will so fill the earth that it will be destroyed! (I know this sounds crazy. I can't believe I'm even writing this, but read II Peter 3:10). The earth is headed for destruction! God must burn up sin!

And yet:

God has made provision to restore order and harmony to His universe!

For this reason, Christ, meaning *"the anointed one"* (Jesus, the Son of God), was born to restore order and redeem back to the Father all that was lost!

What was lost?

- You and me! We were all lost because of *sin* (we all sin and do wrong because we all are descendants of Adam)!
- Man's spiritual connection with God, the Father was severed. Since God is "existence" (life) when Adam sinned, he "died" (became disconnected spiritually). Being cut off from the source of life, he eventually died physically. Therefore, all who are born will one day die (physically), yet, our spirit/soul will continue to live—either with God the Father in heaven (being reconnected to him through our belief in Jesus Christ)—or to burn in hell forever.
- Man could no longer be in fellowship with God and was kicked out of His presence.
- Man was no longer *like* God. Man became increasingly, rebellious, lustful, and wicked). Man has become slaves to sin, and Satan has become man's teacher and guide (instead of God).
- Man became *world conscious* instead of God conscious (focusing on himself and material things rather than on God his creator). Man's sight or ability to perceive the things of God was darkened.
- Man's *spirit (the life/breath within him)* now *"fallen"* (i.e. corrupted)—no longer resembling God's *Holy Spirit (Life, Power)*—began following his *own heart* (i.e. Satan).

Man has fallen into darkness (ignorance) and continues to exist and operate from there.

Sin has separated (and continues to separate) God and man!

Furthermore, sin has reached all the way to the heavens! (Revelation 18:5)

However

God has and is now preparing a new heaven and a new earth for those who believe in Jesus the Christ!

God wants to mend the separation between us (you) and Him!

Why should we believe in Jesus?

Open your eyes…Face the truth!

Jesus is God!
Let's look again at Adam.

God formed Adam from the earth (Adam means "red earth" or "clay") in His image and likeness (to function as He functions—reproducing after Himself, replenishing the earth, subduing it, and having dominion over it). (See Genesis 1:28.)

God *breathed* the *'breath of life'* (His Spirit) into Adam! (See Genesis 2:7.)

God took Eve (the first woman) out of Adam! (See Genesis 2:21-23.)

God gave this command, *"Be fruitful and multiply."* (God told Adam to do physically what He has done spiritually). (See Genesis 1:22.)

God *"spoke"* the universe into existence! God spoke and—BANG! The universe came to be! (The big bang theory is true! *God* said, *"Let there be . . . ,"* and *Bang!* Things started happening!). (Read Genesis 1)

As we discussed in a previous chapter, words are also seeds. Every word carries a good or evil spirit (thought or intention).

As I have stated in previous chapters. When words are spoken or written, finding good ground (a mind willing to receive what was spoken), they begin to grow. When what was planted is fully grown, it will bring forth fruit like itself. This is a continuous cycle!

- God made Adam. Adam was God's first fruit (in the physical).
- Both the man and the woman were called Adam! (Genesis 5:2)
- The man was given physical seed (sperm) to reproduce after his own kind. To bring up Godly children unto God!

"Seed" (within itself) contains all things pertaining to life. As this author stated in a previous chapter, *'seed'* is able to reproduce itself over and over and over again (infinitely)! One seed contains many generations within itself!

Both the man and the woman sinned—and God punished both of them!

- The woman was deceived (by the serpent, who is Satan); she ate of the forbidden tree (the tree of knowledge of good and evil).
- The woman gave to her husband—and he ate.
- They *fell*! The woman however had no *seed* (sperm).
- Sin separated *"Adam"* from God and also separated the man and the woman from each other!

(Read Genesis Chapter 3 of the Holy Bible)

The man carried the seed. (Because Adam's sperm was corrupted when he sinned, corruption was passed down to all generations even until now.)

Adam's sin was devastating! His *fall* was great! He went from perfection to corruption, from brilliant light—to pitch-black darkness! (And we are all Adam's descendants.)

- Adam's seed or sperm was corrupted by his sin. (Sin is rebellion or disobedience.)
- Adam and his wife no longer shared *God's Holy* Spirit. The breath (life, spirit) in man is opposed to God. (The woman was taken out of man and therefore possessed the breath of life.)
- Because we are all descendants of Adam all of mankind are slaves to sin and follow after Satan, *"the Father of lies, "the Evil One"*.

Note: Although Adam still had the "authority" God had given to him, Satan became man's guide and teacher!

Adam's seed continues to become increasingly wicked with each passing generation!

We are Adam's seed, reproducing (evil) after our own kind.

Like in farming, seeds are planted into fertile soil. So also sperm (seed) is planted into a woman's fertile soil (the egg). The egg has all of the nutrients needed to nurture and bring forth life. Sperm breaks through the egg, buries itself into the soil, and dies. The sperm fertilizes the egg and thus creates new life.

Man (who is like God) deposits his sperm (seed) into a woman whose egg is like the earth (soil). This coming together creates something new! What is created is a new being that is a combination of both father (like God) and mother (like the earth)! A beautiful baby is formed!

Once again, since we all are from Adam—we are (all of us) sinners.

Adam's seed was tainted because he sinned, and through his seed, we all are filled with corruption! Rebellion, hatred, bitterness, violence, sexual perversion, addictions, phobias, mental disorders, sickness, disease—and murder all stem from sin. (And that is why we can never obtain freedom from these diseases and disorders on our own! Sin has saturated our bodies; therefore, as long as we are in our bodies, we will—sin.)

Sin hinders our ability to choose right over wrong!

Sin says, *"There are no absolutes! There is nothing that is always right or always wrong. It depends on the situation!"* (But then—sin's statement is proven to be a lie because the statement it spoke was an absolute statement).

This world (the way it functions) is under Satan's influence. We are governed by greed, we are motivated by selfishness and the pursuit of pleasure. We were born into this world with sin (corruption, rebelliousness, wickedness) already in us. Being of this world, we (naturally) go with the flow of the world. We don't know any better! Therefore, we follow the sinful laws and perverse teachings of this world. These are *lust of the eyes, lust of the flesh, and the pride of life.* (See 1 John 2:16.)

The payment for (practicing) sin is death! (See Romans 6:23.)

- Sin is the action caused by an error in judgment, believing and acting on the whispers of an evil spirit or thoughts (gossip, lies, rumors, pride, accusations, and fear).
- The unsaved person is blind to his own wickedness.
- It takes the light and the truth of *God's Word* to find us where we are and to make us aware of ourselves (how hopelessly evil we really are).

- Having seen ourselves through the mirror of God's Word, we are given the opportunity to repent (turn away from our ways and accept God's way), which will afford us life, or we can continue in sin and die!

Jesus the Christ!
(The only begotten Son of God)

Jesus is Lord!
He was with God in the beginning!

In the beginning was the Word, and the Word was with God, and the Word was God. The same was in the beginning with God. All things were made by him; and without him was not anything made that was made. (John 1:1-3.)

Jesus, the God-man

- Jesus is 100% God and 100% man (the Hypostatic Union)!

Seed is passed from father to son. Men are the carriers of '*seed*' or sperm. Jesus' Father (Jehovah) was not a man—but God! Jesus' mother was a virgin when the Holy Spirit overshadowed her—thus, Jesus was conceived in her womb! (See Luke 1:35.)

Babies are a new creation! Babies have the attributes of their fathers as well as those of their mothers, in one precious tiny package!

Babies' blood is that of the father! And the life of a thing is in the blood! (See Leviticus 17:11.) This is why men desire to have sons so that their bloodline will be continued!

Jesus was born to live as our example—and to die in order to restore what was lost by Adam when he sinned. Although Jesus always existed, He was made (physically), the first born of a new creation (being both God and man in one being and being the first to be resurrected from the dead)!

In whom we have REDEMPTION THROUGH HIS BLOOD, even the forgiveness of sins (Jesus) who is THE IMAGE OF THE INVISIBLE GOD, THE FIRST BORN OF EVERY CREATURE: FOR BY HIM WERE ALL THINGS CREATED, that are in heaven, and that are in earth, visible and invisible, whether they be thrones, or dominions, or principalities, or powers: ALL THINGS WERE CREATED BY HIM, AND FOR HIM: and HE IS BEFORE ALL THINGS, AND BY HIM ALL THINGS CONSIST. And he is the head of the church: who is the beginning, THE FIRSTBORN FROM THE DEAD; that in all things he might have preeminence. (Colossians 1:14-18)—Emphasis added

Jesus is the *"Word" of God*—made flesh!

Although He was and is flesh (like man), the sin nature of man was not obeyed because His Father's nature was present to assist and empower Him. Once again, Jesus was fully man—and fully God; having two natures (one natural and one spiritual). Therefore, He was able to live a sinless life!

Jesus was born *free* to make a choice. He *CHOSE* not to follow what his *flesh* wanted to do! (Read Matthew 4:1-11.)

Although sin was in His flesh (the outer man, through his mother), it was not in His *heart* (where the *spirit*, the breath of life is centered). Thus, He was able to live (without sinning)!

Jesus knew who He was and He knew His purpose!

Jesus' inner man was in control!

This is not so with man. Man's spirit is disconnected from God and therefore, He (GOD) considers us (spiritually) dead. Our inner man has no control. As long as we remain unsaved, we will have no connection with God and will die in our sins (not being forgiven). *If* we die in our sins, God will judge us! He will not receive us because we have _NOT_ been reconnected to Him. We therefore _DO NOT_ belong to Him.

We need to be saved! We need a Savior! (But who can save us from ourselves?)

Only Jesus Christ, the Son of God, can save us! He will save everyone that believes and calls upon His name (but this is not merely a one-time call—this "calling" is for a lifelong relationship)!

Jesus, whose blood was holy (God's), offered Himself as the sinless sacrifice to redeem and restore man to his rightful place with God.

Innocent blood was shed to cover and cancel out the damage done by sin and sin's mastery over us!

The unsaved are actually slaves to sin!

There is no way that the unsaved person can free himself or herself from the power and authority of sin. Sin dominates the unsaved person's life completely!

In general, people only think of sins that we can see with our eyes or commit physically—God however, looks at those sins we see and those sins that are unseen! Hidden hatred, anger, jealousy, bitterness, self-righteousness, greed, slander, judging (condemning), prejudices and other such issues of the heart that we fail to consider and or tend to mask, are clearly seen, noted—and will be judged by God.

Only those who have called on the name of Jesus, believing in their *hearts* that God has raised Him from the dead, are given power to overcome their sin nature (John 1:12). This is because when they (truly) believed and confessed that Jesus is Lord, God placed His *Holy Spirit* within them—restoring that original *'breath of life'* that was corrupted when Adam sinned. (2 Corinthians 1:22). The Holy Spirit is given to believers as a seal, separating us to God and from those whom He will judge. He (the Holy Spirit) is the proof of salvation to those who have believed! The fruit of the Spirit is kindness, self-control, joy, peace, patience, endurance, and love! (See Galatians 5:22-25.)

By believing that Jesus is Lord, that His blood was shed for the forgiveness of all sin and that the Father raised Him from the dead, we become as adopted sons of God and share in Jesus' inheritance with Him forever! (See Romans 8:15.)

Open your eyes…Face the truth!

Those that have been saved have passed from death to life!

The Holy Spirit makes what was dead, alive! (See Genesis 2:7 and John 6:63.)

Now that we are saved, we are given help and power (ability) to change the direction of our thinking (thus changing our actions). (See Philippians 2:13.)

The thoughts of the unsaved and unbelievers are polluted through and through!

- One's judgments are made through one's own twisted thoughts and experiences (what was taught, seen, heard—or derived by experience).
- Many people are self-righteous. What looks, seems or feels good to such a person is good (in the eyes of that person) and what is bad in (that same person's eyes) is bad.
- Right and wrong have no absolutes or rather, they are seen as relative—given the situation. As stated earlier, they are both subject to change according to the situation or circumstances.

Example:

A woman who is cheating on her husband would be judged as wrong in God's sight! Yet—if this woman's husband was abusive and or a cheater, many of us would say, *"She's justified."* (God would still judge her as wrong)! Others might say, *"She's wrong—but . . ."* (See? No absolutes). This is the thinking of those who have NO STANDARD of right or wrong! God has given us the Bible, His standard of right and wrong! *His Word* is the absolute truth. We gain knowledge of Jesus through the reading of *His Word.*

Sin is very deceitful! One may believe one has conquered one's habit or addiction but sin only retreats or hides, reappearing in another form. For example, one may quit smoking crack or doing heroin. One may be quite happy with this accomplishment but a closer look at this person's life may reveal cigarette addiction, overeating or pride (self-righteousness, a critical spirit, and arrogance)! Only by giving ourselves wholly to God, by believing and following the teachings of Jesus Christ, can we truly be cleansed of sin, and that in itself is a process!

When we receive the Spirit of Christ in our hearts, we are reborn or "born again"; our spirit is renewed or made alive! We must receive Christ by believing that God sent Him to be the only (worthy) sacrifice that will blot out all of our sins so that we may be reconnected to the Father. Like a newborn baby, we need to be taught how to live (as God would have us to live). It is by reading the Bible (God's Word) that we gain knowledge, wisdom and understanding.

God's Word, the Bible, is the instruction manual for our new life! Apply it and live; ignore it and reap the consequences.

Like buying a new car, computer, iPod or video game system, most people never read the instruction manual (bible) once they become believers. Because of their lack of knowledge, they go through trial and error, needless confusion, pain, and suffering. Countless people have lost their lives because they did not read and then follow the instructions. Some of us only read the instructions in part. Although we experience some successful results, we never come to experience total life! (This is a shameful reality). Then there are those individuals who are thieves and robbers, who (like those who steal cable) seemingly enjoy the benefits of a *false salvation* (not truly believing or making Jesus master of their lives). Their pleasure will be cut off suddenly and their punishment will be severe!

God's Word is a mirror, showing the *born again* believer (in Christ) all of the junk that is in us!

When God reveals this junk to us, He then gives us a choice. God urges us to give our mess over to Him:

- That He may destroy it, replacing it with something new and pure.
- That we may be healed and delivered (of sickness, disease, addictions, bad habits, and strongholds, which are patterns of behavior or thought).

If we deny *God's Word*, we are (literally) telling Him that *"I like this. I don't want to be healed. I don't want to be delivered!"*

God, in turn, will allow us to remain in that state. As sin continues to cause destruction in our lives, God will ask over and over again, *"Do you love me more than this (habit or destructive way of thinking)?"* If we answer yes, God will begin to remove the root of sin in our lives, one by one and sin by sin. If our answer is No God will allow sin to run its course. Our condition will continue to get worse!

Our every action has infinite reactions!

The actions of one individual affect the actions and reactions of everyone else. (We are all linked, and we come from one source—God!)

Actions done according to God's will are fruitful and beneficial to all!

Proud, rebellious, and selfish acts cause harm, divisions, corruption, and eventually, death!

Warning:

The proud and arrogant will be made to fall! (And everyone will see it!)

Finally, the Bible clearly states . . .

"As it is written: THERE IS NO ONE RIGHTEOUS, NOT EVEN ONE; THERE IS NO ONE WHO UNDERSTANDS, NO ONE WHO SEEKS GOD. (Romans 3:10-11, NIV).

"FOR ALL HAVE SINNED and come short of the glory of God" (Romans 3:23, KJV).

"FOR GOD LOVED THE WORLD THAT HE GAVE HIS ONE AND ONLY SON, THAT WHOEVER BELIEVES IN HIM SHALL NOT PERISH BUT HAVE ETERNAL LIFE" (John 3:16, NIV).

"But God demonstrates his own love for us in this: WHILE WE WERE STILL SINNERS, CHRIST DIED FOR US" (Romans 5:8, NIV).

"THAT IF YOU CONFESS WITH YOUR MOUTH, 'JESUS IS LORD,' AND BELIEVE IN YOUR HEART THAT GOD RAISED HIM FROM THE DEAD,

YOU WILL BE SAVED. For it is with your heart that you believe and are justified, and it is with your mouth that you confess and are saved" (Romans 10:9-10, NIV).

"Jesus answered, 'I AM THE WAY AND THE TRUTH AND THE LIFE. NO ONE COMES TO THE FATHER EXCEPT THROUGH ME" (John 14:6, NIV).

"Salvation is found in no one else, FOR THERE IS NO OTHER NAME UNDER HEAVEN GIVEN TO MEN BY WHICH WE MUST BE SAVED" (Acts 4:12, NIV).

Don't continue to live a life of destruction.

Believe!

Love!
(There is no greater power!)

Love is the key! Love is the solution! Love is the power!

Love conquers all!

Love has the power to heal our mental and emotional wounds!

There is a saying that states, *"Time heals all wounds"—this* is an untrue statement! If time truly healed all wounds, there would be no alcoholics, no bitterness, no deep-rooted fears and phobias, no hate, etc. A better statement would be to say that…

"Love heals all wounds!" **This is because only 'love' has the ability to tear down strongholds and destroys the yokes of bondage.**

*Strongholds are destructive patterns of thinking that have grown so powerful that they control the entire person).

*Bondage is slavery of any kind (i.e. behaviors, habits and illness and/or disease that build up and spring from the stronghold).

But what is love?

Love may not be what you are accustomed to thinking!

"God is love"! (1 John 4:8)

"Love covers a multitude of sins," and ***"Perfect love casts out all fears."*** (1 John 4:18 and 1 Peter 4:8)

Since God is love, then the statement "Love heals all wounds" holds true! How else can we explain such drastic changes as that of juvenile delinquents (for example) whom everyone (even family) had given up on—doing a total about face (from violent, rebellious hoodlums—to model citizens)? The answer: someone took hold of them and loved them! Those persons were shown genuine love (through action) and that gave them the desire to change! Those boys and girls were shown patience and kindness, mentored, counseled, listened to, cared for—and given time, space and room to grow and learn. They were *shown* love. They saw love in action; felt it! And what they were shown, in time, they received and embraced!

Need I mention those persons who have been completely delivered from various fears and addictions? If we could rewind and witness the process of their deliverance, we would find that someone showed them love! It was, after all, the lack of *'love'* or perverted love that shaped them into who they were (previously). There is something about genuine love that soothes, heals and encourages as well as *"casts out all of our fears"* (insecurities, worries, anxieties, doubts and concerns).

Commercial: Before we continue with this discussion on love, I feel it necessary to distinguish four forms of love.

1. *Godly love-* (perfect love) which extends from God (the Father) toward us—and encompasses both brotherly love and family love.
2. *Brotherly love*, which is the kindly, friendly affection that we express toward one another (charity)
3. *Family love-* which is the supportive, caring, nurturing concern about those who are related to us (father, mother, brother, sister, cousins, etc.)
4. *Eros-* sensual or physical love (dealing with sex)

If perfect love was given to us (through our parents) and embraced by *all* of us—Dad and or Mom would not have:

- Walked out (never to return)
- Been abusive
- Cheated
- Gotten a divorce
- Abused drugs/alcohol

Friends, family members—and we would not be:

- Embittered (resentful)
- Jealous
- Disrespectful
- Selfish
- Slanderous (talking about and tearing down others)
- Impatient and critical toward others.
- No one would have low *self-esteem*;
- there would be no fear or hate

… Love would rule (in our hearts)! We would love one another as we would a brother or a sister!

Unfortunately, *sin* (disobedience or wrongdoing) has kept us from (truly) loving one another since the start of mankind. Our ancestors' great-grandparents and their great-grandparents'—grandparents have *sinned*. Their sins continue to affect us to this day! We were born in sin (with disobedience, selfishness, pride, perverseness, sickness and disease already inside of us). This is a result of the sins committed by our ancestors even as far back as the first man (Adam)!

Therefore, love is often hindered by *pride* (man's selfishness) and fear!

You might be asking yourself, *"If God is love and He is supposed to be all-powerful, how can He be hindered?*

God has given *'free will'* to every one of us. He is not hindered! It is we who push away and reject what *He* is attempting to bestow upon us. We are the hindrance! We hinder ourselves (from being helped, healed and delivered) because we choose not to accept *His love*. (We will go deeper into this later.)

Love must be received—as a gift—in order for (love's) power to successfully affect us!

"Love suffers long, and is kind; love does not envy; love does not parade itself, is not puffed up; does not behave rudely, does not seek its own, is not provoked, thinks no evil; does not rejoice in iniquity, but rejoices in the truth; bears all things, believes all things, hopes all things, endures all things. Love never fails …" (1 Corinthians 13:4-8, NKJV)

Love is _NOT_ a feeling!

Genuine love does not stop or shut off—because you or *"I don't feel like it"* or *"no longer feel the same."*

Those who are led by their emotions act in the following manner. They tend to jump from relationship to relationship, from job to job and from one mood to the next (depending on what they feel). They are reactionary. They *'react'* to whatever is going on in their environment. If it is sunny—then they are happy! If it rains—they are miserable. They go up and down as the wind blows. If the conditions of their environment change (their partner loses his or her job for example; becomes ill or is unable to make them happy), they are greatly affected and will eventually jump ship! Such people prove to be unreliable, flighty and fickle. They are *"…unstable in all their ways!"* (James 1:8)

***"Love is a decision. That decision is to seek another person's highest good (despite how we are treated in return)."*—Dr. Walter L. Swinson**

In other words, love seeks to make the other person—better. Love wants to make sure that the other person has food, clothes, shelter, peace of mind, comfort, stability—and whatever else is needed to insure the other person's well-being.

See? When we look at 'love' in this manner, we are forced to admit that we really don't "love" as we should.

Love—never fails!

Because the *source* of love is from God (who is infinite and inexhaustible in power), it never runs out! The problem is, we (humans) do not remain connected to God—our source (through prayer and obedience to Him). Therefore, we run out of love and have to go to God to be refilled. If we were to cultivate a strong relationship with *the Father*—through prayer and living a life that is pleasing to Him, we would soon conclude that the following statements are true!

Love is pure; it has neither limitations nor boundaries! Love never runs out!

Love is always growing and expanding!

God is love (and every pure expression of love extends from Him)!

Love is the beginning and the ending of 'understanding'.

Because love delves deep below the surface (into our very hearts), love can see our true state and the cause (or causes) of our condition! Love—using this insight (into our true thoughts and intentions) begins to deal with us at the root of our issues and thus bring forth whatever we stand in need of (healing, deliverance, etc.).

When we express love, we are literally allowing ourselves to be used by God!

We are allowing ourselves to be used as a vessel; as God pours Himself into us—we pour that same love out on others!

When we are not displaying love, we are acting out in selfishness and pride.
The Holy Spirit is *the power* of love! It is the Holy Spirit that enters our hearts and empowers us to love (do the will of God).

The Holy Spirit is the *Spirit of God*—and He *is* God! He is sent from God (the Father) to awaken to our *dead spirits* (that were disconnected from Him) and to live in our hearts. The Holy Spirit helps us to love! He gives us the desire to worship and to acknowledge God, shows us the way of love and teaches us to live unselfishly, seeking the highest good for others!

That is why the Lord Jesus Christ is so important! If it were not for His sacrifice, we would not be able to comprehend God's great love toward us!

God (the Father), seeking our highest good—sent His Son, Jesus (meaning Jehovah is salvation) into the world to show us what love is supposed to look like and—moreover to die for us, so that our sins (which caused our disconnection from God)—would be forgiven. Jesus died so that we can be reconnected to the Father!

"But God demonstrates His love toward us, in that while we were still sinners, Christ died for us!" (Romans 5:8, NKJV)

A few people would die to save the life of a good man, but Christ died to save all men!

"For God so loved the world that He gave His only begotten Son that whosoever shall believe in him shall not perish but have everlasting life." (John 3:16)

The Holy Spirit will not enter in and dwell in those who do not believe or accept the Lord Jesus into their hearts. The Holy Spirit comes to us only through our acknowledgment of Christ's finished work (dying on the cross) and our holding on to the truth (that God raised him from the dead) in our hearts. So then, we that believe "love him because he first loved us!" (1 John 4:19) And we should love as *He* loves—unselfishly!

God desires to use us (those who have accepted the Lord Jesus Christ in their hearts) to show others His goodness! God (the Father) is invisible to us; therefore, He uses believers in Him to live by example—before others. Jesus—once again—is significant because without his coming in the flesh, we would never have an example of what God's personality is like—and how he behaves!

The problem is and has always been—us! As long as we continue to believe and obey God's commands (the Bible), love's power will continue to heal and free us from our hurts, sicknesses and addictions. It is when we choose to disobey that we fall back or hurt others.

This world system (the government and the way the world functions) will be destroyed because 'love' has no place in it!

Selfishness, greed and pride have so polluted this world and have so blinded its people that they reject 'love'. They want nothing to do with love because they want no parts of God. ***God is love!*** He is unwelcome, even hated, in the hearts of those He has created!

Rather than destroy the world and everyone in it, God—being full of mercy, has given us all the opportunity to be saved from His coming wrath! By sending His son Jesus (love in human form) into the world! God extends this invitation:

If anyone believes that God (Love) has sent His son Jesus into the world to die for our sins and confesses that Jesus is Lord; believing that the power of love has raised him from the dead—that person shall receive love (the Holy Spirit of God) in his heart and shall be saved from the coming judgment. What is the coming judgment? The coming judgment is to be cast into hell to burn and be forever—separated from God (Love).

Without love, there is no peace (individually or otherwise)!

Without love there is no true freedom!

Love is freedom!

Despite what we have been taught, love is an attribute that is a part of being masculine!

Love is a trait that has its beginnings in the masculine and is continued and sustained in the feminine!

- God is the source of all things
- God is the *Father*, meaning *"source."* It is from the father's seed that sparks and starts all things!
  - Masculine (love) plants the seed (sperm)
  - Feminine (love) carries, nurtures, and brings forth what was planted

Open your eyes…Face the truth!

A woman's motivation: To receive love (Listen to their language)! "I just want someone to love me!"

*Young girls, looking for love, may become pregnant (on purpose) because they desire to receive the unconditional love that a baby will give to them.

Man's motivation: (Listen to his language) "I just want someone to love!

Love (how it functions)—has become twisted.

Presently, males are too selfish to give—*love*. Many of us (males) are trying desperately to hold on to our macho or thuggish image—rather than express (love). It has been deemed uncool, soft and weak to express love—so most (immature) men don't.

In stark contrast, women have become too hard, conceited and critical to receive *love* when it approaches them.

Both sexes have trouble perceiving "Love" because we (as individuals) are self-centered. We are in love with ourselves. We have a perverted form of love that is self-seeking, self-gratifying and self-absorbed, (i.e. lust).

The giver is always stronger than the receiver!

Man is God's representative in the earth! Man's job was to name the animals, dress the garden, subdue the earth, shaping and forming it into more than what it was (Genesis 2). Women take what men give, helping him by caring for what was sown. Women manage, nourish, comfort and care for—that is what they do (when they are functioning correctly). Although these attributes are shown by both parents, the man is hardwired to be a visionary, leader, provider and protector, while the woman is the nurturer and caregiver.

A healthy family functions in this manner!

Man and woman working together as a team, complimenting one another, flowing in perfect harmony—this too, is *love*. (This is how God operates: *The Father* is the source and makes the plan; *Jesus the Son* carries out the plan; and the *Holy Spirit* holds, sustains, and nurtures the finished work!)

218

God is love! He sent His son (Jesus) into the world to establish love and the Holy Spirit is sent into the world to gather those who would believe in God's love and then to maintain love until God brings His followers to be with Him. Eventually, He will overthrow all of the unbelievers—and those that oppose love!

Husbands are told to love their wives because in doing so, they are imitating their Father—God!

Sin has twisted our nature!

We were fearfully and wonderfully made (by, through and for—love)!

Men were created to love (in a certain manner)—but we are currently being taught to hide it, to be unfeeling, to withhold it—some men even admit that they *fear* (love).

Perfect 'love' cast out all fear!

Women were made to receive love—but they are taught to exploit it, to use their bodies and charms to get what they desire. Sadly, increasing numbers of woman believe that 'love' is shown by what they can get—materialistically. They feel that if they are not showered with gifts—they are not being loved.

More and more, it is the men that are becoming the receivers—while women are the givers. Women are taking care of men—and the men are sitting at home expecting to receive gifts.

Presently, even the very natures of men and woman have and are becoming twisted. Men are becoming effeminate, women are becoming masculine! (I speak of homosexuality, lesbianism and same sex marriages. Read Romans Chapter 1)

In the last days... because iniquity shall abound, the love of many shall wax cold. (Matthew 24:12)

Open your eyes...Face the truth!

Think about it! Sin is destroying the family structure and has been rapidly gaining ground into our homes. Because of this pollution, each generation has become colder, harder and more wicked (twisted). *What is the pollution that I speak of?*

When fathers are absent from their families or fail to show love, the result is bitterness, rebellion, perversion, etc. Their children may become selfish and hateful, which is the opposite of love.

Did you know that it is the same outcome when mothers are dysfunctional or absent?

"Hate" is love—that has been rejected, hurt or has become jealous! (We've said this before.)

- Someone we love rejects us- our emotions toward them may become negative, desiring that they suffer (as we have suffered).
- Someone hurts our feelings- we desire for them to hurt—and we desire revenge.
- Jealousy- hatred toward someone because they possess something that we do not have—but desire the thing or things for ourselves.

(All of the above stems from *a lack of love*.)

Satan has been blinding and distracting us so that we cannot act in *love*. He has perverted, polluted and continues to suppress *love*. If Satan cannot push us into hate and callousness and bind us there, he tries pulls us into the deep waters of *lust* and *perversion*. Most people cannot discern what *love* really looks like or how (love) moves, responds or behaves. For instance, (in past times) men have been encouraged to be rugged, strong and silent. However (presently) increasing numbers of men are effeminate—seeking the love and affection of other men. This behavior is also increasing in our women. It is in part, because the *'love'* that was shown them or that they have experienced was 'twisted'—or absent altogether.

"God is love"! (1 John 4:8)

God is our *Father* and He wants to restore us back to our rightful place in Him (Love)!

The reconnection to *God, the Father* can only be established by receiving the Lord Jesus in our hearts and then committing ourselves to the following of his teachings.

I believe I have mentioned the following statement in a previous chapter:

"It is difficult for young men to see God because many have not received love from their fathers. It is a foreign concept to them! They find it hard to believe that a masculine God loves them and wants to have a relationship with them. They see God in the same way that they look at their own fathers—uncaring, absent, and a big disappointment! They do not believe and are determined to live without Him!" (Dr. Walter Swinson)

Young women are willing to receive God more readily than young men; however, they often relate to God in the same manner they relate to the men in their lives. They will attempt to manipulate God through service (offering their bodies in order to get something they want), begging and crying (hoping God will cave in), and flattery (speaking empty words). Few have any intention, however, of submitting themselves to God's authority! Once they receive what they have desired from God, they might <u>NOT</u> acknowledge Him again until they need or want something else!

Love is selfless!

With each passing generation, love is increasingly rejected!

Imagine what would happen if we were to show real *love* to our children. The sky would be their limit! I have heard that scientist have made studies concerning both babies and children; they have shown love and nurturing to one group and deprived the other. The results—I hear—were that the group that received loved—thrived! The groups that did not receive love suffered in their health, learning, became delinquent and some of the babies—died. (I have not done the research on this personally and do not claim this to be the truth).

This we do know! If a child is deprived of love, that child will neither recognize nor display love when he or she becomes an adult. If he or she does recognize love he or she will not readily respond to (love).

Neither man nor woman will know or appreciate love if they have grown up and have not been (loved). Love is an unfamiliar concept to such a person. Although one may have seen love displayed toward others and may long for (love)—this individual will not recognize or receive love when it comes to them. Such a person's nature will cause him or her to—not only fear love but also to fight against it—attempting to drive it off. He or she may desire to be loved—yet it is not in his or her capacity to accept it. Such an individual views love through his or her experiences and how he or she would act. They wish to control love and force love to act as they wish (love) to behave. Because love is unfamiliar and strange to him or her, he or she does not trust (love) because he or she does not understand the motivation behind it! In time, love's continuous kindness may win the heart of such an individual— but he or she must be willing to open his or her heart to receive love. If that person is unwilling to trust (because he or she *fears* he or she will appear foolish or because he or she doesn't want to lose control)—love might eventually move on—allowing that person to continue with *selfish* pursuits that will amount to nothing. Such an individual will continue in loneliness and emptiness—unless he or she can change their response to love. In such a case, love may never return to them.

(I am speaking of love—as it relates to God—friendships, family and potential soul mates.)

With love, there is life and peace! Selfishness leads to personal loss, loneliness and possibly self-destruction.

He that does not love does not know God, *for God is Love.* (I John 4:7)

God is love! Accept the love of God by receiving the Lord Jesus into your heart!

"Beloved, if God so loved us, we ought also to love one another." (I John 4:11)

Do to others as you would have them do to you. (Luke 6:31)

Love must be sincere. Hate what is evil, cling to what is good. (Romans 12:9)

Love does no harm to a neighbor. Therefore love is the fulfillment of the law. (roman13:10)

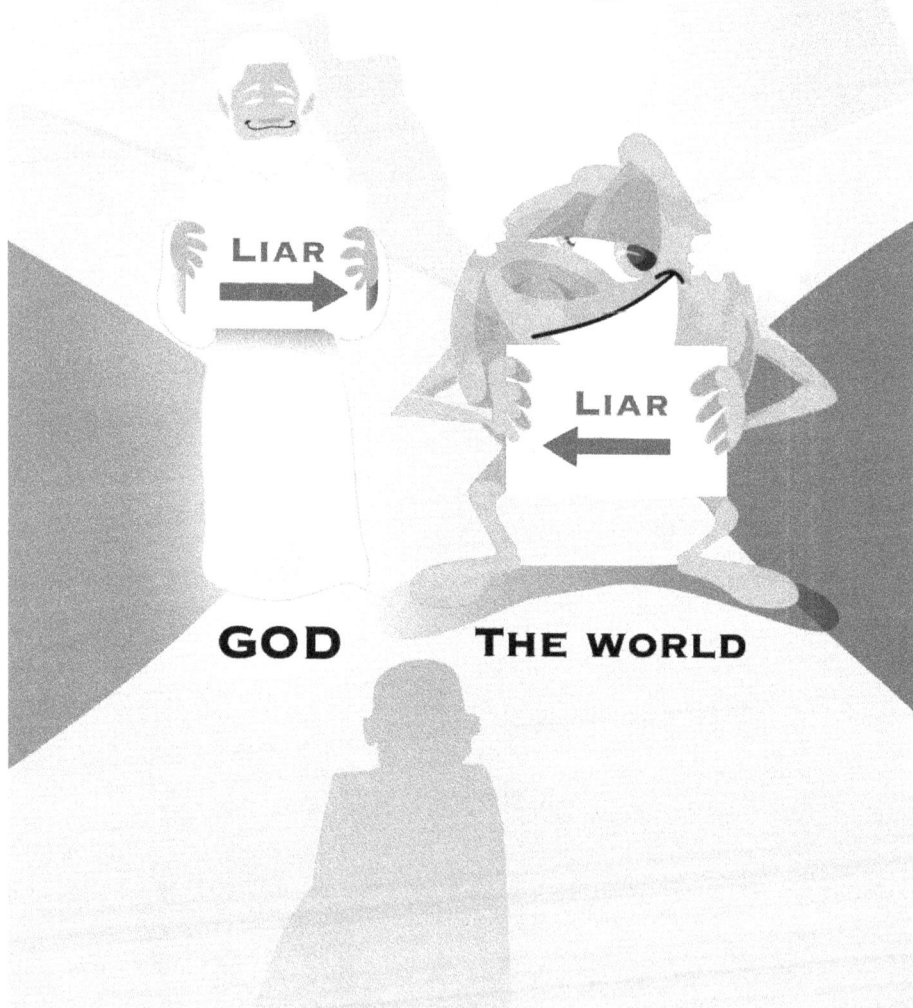

It's Your Choice

Now, my friend, we are standing at the crossroads! You have a decision to make. This is the most important decision that you will ever make! On the one hand, you have the truth, which leads to life (everlasting) and peace; on the other hand, you have the way of the world, which leads to death and destruction. Choose the truth—and God will place His Holy Spirit in you-- who will begin to process you, cleansing and freeing you from the various habits, addictions and strongholds that have been destroying us all! Choose the world and continue in ignorance, selfishness, pride, greed, violence and in the things that cause pain, sickness and disease, strife, suicide and murder!

What will you choose? Are you still not convinced? Perhaps you like the way you are and the way things are going in your life. Yet—if this was truth, you would not have read this book—and (since you have read this far) you are held accountable! One day, you will stand before the God of the universe! He will ask you, *"Why didn't you believe?"* My friend, you are without excuse. If you choose the way of the world, you will be choosing to go to hell (where you will be eternally separated from God)!

Perhaps you are thinking, *"There must be another way to reach heaven."* Well—there isn't. There is no other way except that one comes through Jesus, the Christ! Let me explain through the following illustration:

Let's say, you are throwing the biggest, most extravagant party ever! (Even Sean "Diddy" Combs is overcome with awe)! Let's say that you have spared no expense! You have hung the best decorations, the finest foods have been prepared, the finest drinks will be served, and the invitations have been printed up and sent out. This party is going to be the Godzilla of all parties! All other parties before and after this one are just gatherings of cupcakes and Kool-Aid! (Get the picture?)

Now, let's say that you have placed your best (and trusted) friend at the door as the greeter, telling him or her that *"Whoever you let in is welcome. Whoever is cool with you is cool with me! Just make sure that you stamp everyone's hand as a sign that they were invited."*

Hours later, the party is in full swing! There are more guests than you can shake a stick at—yet you intend to meet and greet every single person. (A gracious host makes it his or her point to personally recognize everyone that attends their functions.) Consequently, you go to your friend, and together the two of you greet every guest. After some time, you come to a person or group of persons that your friend does not recognize. *"I don't remember letting them in!"* your friend tells you. What then would you do! These persons are dressed incorrectly, their actions are out of sorts and upon inspection you find that they do not have the stamp (of approval) on their hands! These persons have crashed the party—*your party!* You will without a doubt throw those gate crashers out on their tails (and you would be justified in doing so!).

Now check this out!

This is exactly what God is preparing to do to those who attempt to get into heaven (the party) without going through or meeting the man at the door (or rather *is* "the door")! He—that is the door—is Jesus Christ, the only begotten son of God, who stamps or seals us with His Holy Spirit—who serves as our proof (before God) that we are invited guests! All those that are not "sealed" and attempt to crash the (heavenly) party will be thrown out! The place prepared for those gate crashers (those thieves and robbers) is *hell and the lake of fire* where they will burn forever!

I am not making this up. Look at what the Bible says concerning this matter!

The Parable of the Wedding Banquet-Matthew 22:14 (NIV)

Jesus spoke to them again in parables, saying: 2 "The kingdom of heaven is like a king who prepared a wedding banquet for his son. 3 He sent his servants to those who had been invited to the banquet to tell them to come, but they refused to come. 4 "Then he sent some more servants and said, 'Tell those who have been invited that I have prepared my dinner: My oxen and fattened cattle have been butchered, and everything is ready. Come to the wedding banquet.' 5 "But they paid no attention and went off—one to his field, another to his business. 6 The rest seized his servants, mistreated them and killed them. 7 The king was enraged. He sent his army and destroyed those murderers and burned their city. 8 "Then he said to his servants, 'The wedding banquet is ready, but those I invited did not deserve to come. 9 So go to the street corners and invite to the banquet anyone you find.' 10 So the servants went out into the streets and gathered all the people they could find, the bad as well as the good, and the wedding hall was filled with guests. 11 "But when the king came in to see the guests, he noticed a man there who was not wearing wedding clothes. 12 He asked, 'How did you get in here without wedding clothes, friend?' The man was speechless. 13 "Then the king told the attendants, 'Tie him hand and foot, and throw him outside, into the darkness, where there will be weeping and gnashing of teeth.' 14 "For many are invited, but few are chosen."

My friend, (today) you have come to a fork in the road. There is one path, which leads to death and destruction; and there is another path, which leads to life and peace. The path that leads to destruction is very wide, and on it, you find 'glitz and glamour' (bling-bling, greed) and the 'lusts' of this life. These are the things that look good, feel good and smell fine—yet (in actuality) are empty and unprofitable. This road is littered with the sexually immoral and worshippers of money, clothes and things that we cannot take with us when we die! The mentality of those who tread this path is, *"Life is short, I'm going to get mine,"* not realizing that material things are temporary and that as fast as it came, it can be taken away! The truth is that these people are literally tricked into killing themselves. They get sick, catch diseases, get depressed, drive themselves crazy, rob, steal, lie and commit murder, chasing after things that don't last! Many die in misery, lonely, empty, painfully, violently and all too often—at a young age!

My friend, choose the path (the way) of life! On this path there is peace, love, strong relationships and favor. People will bless you and speak highly of you, they show you kindness, you will receive gifts you did not ask for and you will find that your needs are being met in miraculous ways. There is also wisdom, understanding, freedom and long life—(and when you die physically, your spirit will live forever with the Father God and His son Jesus, the Christ--who is eternally Lord of all. Amen).

Someone once said that life is 10 percent of what happens to us and 90 percent how we (choose) to react! We may not be able to choose what happens to us, our environment, or our circumstances; however, we can choose how we respond! In the end, almost everything is about choice!

Choose wisely!

Open your eyes…Face the truth!

A little encouragement…

I speak words of wisdom.
Pure truth is what I give 'em
Setting youth ablaze…
With courage to keep livin'!
It's a jail break—kid!
We're 'bout to bounce out of prison!
Negativity's risen…
We must remain driven…
…for excellence!
Meditate on these poetics!
Don't get caught up…
…in the sex, drugs or violence epidemic!
(YO!)The odds have been stacked against us…
…don't forget it!!
Get knowledge! Go to college!!
Take heed to this message!
A mind is a terrible thing to waste.
The punishment for doing evil is…
A terrible thing to face!
Live to learn and learn to "love"!
Get the wisdom and understanding…
…that comes from above!
My brother, my sister…
…the struggle continues!
Remember, hard times come…
…to spark the "greatness" within you!

Written by: I. L. Jackson

Bibliography

Drug and alcohol information

(Various drug and alcohol pamphlets) The national Clearinghouse for Alcohol and Drug Information

"Ecstasy and Predatory Drugs" Drug Enforcement Administration www.dea.gov

"Here's Looking At You" 2000 (7th Grade Drug/Alcohol curriculum)

Slave, Fathers

Willie Lynch Letter and Making of a Slave Lushena Books, Lushenabks@yahoo.com

Anger and Conflict Resolution

Handouts and worksheets received from various Prevention trainings. (Previous sources unknown)

Fear, stress (responses) and where otherwise indicated

Christian Education Ministries (Biblical Counseling [course notes]) - Dr. Walter Swinson

Bible references

The Holy Bible, (King James Version, New King James Version, English Standard Version, Berean Literal translation, New International Version)

The New Strong's Exhaustive Concordance of the Bible, Thomas Nelson Publishers

All other insights and observations were provided through interactions with youth (K-12 grades) in the Philadelphia Public School system, with people (in general) and personal experiences examined through the Word of God!

Open your eyes…Face the truth!